NATIVE AMERICANS

cooperative learning activities*

by Susan Schneck and Mary Strohl

*Lessons easily adaptable to traditional classroom or workstation settings

SCHOLASTIC
PROFESSIONAL BOOKS

New York • Toronto • London • Auckland • Sydney

About the Authors

Susan Schneck and Mary Strohl have many years' combined experience in education and publishing. In 1986 they started their own studio, *Flights of Fancy*, specializing in children's activity products and elementary teaching materials. This is their third title for Scholastic Professional Books.

Months of research have gone into making this book about Native Americans. We hope it is only a stepping stone, a beginning, to asking questions and finding more information in the myriad of books about the many cultures and traditions. Your state Bureau of Indian Affairs will have materials you may order for the classroom.

Special Thanks to

Dr. Jay Miller and **Mr. David Edmunds,** Acting Director
Newberry Library, D'Arcy McNickle Center for the History of the American Indian
Chicago, Illinois

Mr. Salvatore J. Natoli, Director of Publications
National Council for the Social Studies
Washington, DC

Dr. Karen D. Harvey, Author
Native American Recipes for the Classroom
Littleton, OH

Ms. Jane T. Edwards, Curator
Mitchell Indian Museum
Evanston, IL

Ms. Sharon Metz, Director
Honor Our Neighbors Origins and Rights, Inc.
Milwaukee, WI

Ms. Donna Beckstrom, Chair
Milwaukee Indian Education Committee, Inc.
Milwaukee, WI

ISBN 0-590-49151-2

12 11 10 9 8 7 6 5 4 3 2 1   1 2 3 4 5/9

TABLE OF CONTENTS

USING THE ACTIVITIES IN THIS BOOK

The purpose of this book is twofold:
- To provide rich information on the day-to-day lives of pre-Colonial Native Americans
- To organize easy-to-follow guidelines for using cooperative learning techniques in your classroom

Each chapter contains background information on the various cultures of the tribes being studied. Introduce these materials prior to beginning group lessons. Look over the text and verify any unfamiliar vocabulary words you may need to introduce to groups. Nonreaders should have the information read to them. If possible, tape the stories on cassette for easy reference. Reproduce the pages for older readers to use in groups.

If you are unfamiliar with cooperative techniques, see the appendix in the back of the book for pointers and for a more detailed key to the recipe symbols shown with each lesson. Cooperative symbols at the beginning of each activity will tell you how to organize groups and how they will proceed. Beside the symbols social skills, academic skills, and teacher directions are provided.

See the appendix in the back of the book for:
- Cooperative learning overview and classroom guidelines
- Social skill descriptions and teaching techniques
- Cooperative recipe descriptions and symbols
- Reproducible classroom management charts and role badges
- Reproducible reward certificate

ABOUT THIS BOOK

Native Americans have lived all across the United States and Canada for thousands of years, long before Christopher Columbus made his voyages across the Atlantic to the "New World." He mistakenly called the people he found living there Indians. Columbus thought he had sailed across the Atlantic to the shores of India. Now we call Indians Native Americans because they were here first, before the colonists came from Europe.

Let's go back about four hundred years to discover what North America was like before the European colonists arrived. We're going to learn about Native Americans and how they survived and flourished in a land that was very different than it is today. They knew how to live well in their environment. People of the Northeast tanned deer hides into soft leather for clothing. They made warm blankets from rabbit fur. They invented snowshoes so they would not sink into the snow in winter. Vast birch forests provided them with bark to make lightweight canoes for transportation on rivers. The Hopi in the Southwest grew crops of corn and cotton in the valleys below their villages. They made things grow in the arid deserts where only grasses and cacti had grown before. Native Americans traded goods among tribes to get materials they could not provide for themselves. You are going to learn about their rich cultures and traditions.

Now imagine you are living four hundred years ago. Take a look at the landscape first. Imagine what your world looks like. There are no big towns or cities; no stores or schools. There are no malls or grocery stores; no roads, cars, trains or planes. You and your family are on your own. If you need something, you have to make it or find it yourselves. Each tribe lives differently because they have to use what is on hand to make everything they need to live. The climate, trees, plants, and animals of the area all influence how you live.

You're going to explore life among Native Americans by meeting six children from different areas of the country. They are going to tell you stories about themselves and their families, clans, and tribes.

- •**Dancing Squirrel** is an Ojibwa boy living in the Northeast.
- •**Golden Fawn** is an Iroquois girl who also lives in the Northeast.
- •**White Clay**, a Cherokee boy, lives in the mountains of what is now North Carolina and Tennessee.
- •**Tall Grass Waving** is a Sioux girl living on the Great Plains in the center of the continent.
- •**Rain in Her Hair** is a Hopi girl Indian from the Pueblo tribe. She lives on a high mesa near the Painted Desert in the Southwest.
- •**Raven's Beak** lives in the rainy but warm Northwest on the western shore of Vancouver Island. He is of the Nootka tribe.

There are hundreds of tribes across the country, but you are going to study six of them. Many of their customs are very similar to other tribes in their area of the country. You will explore with your teammates to discover many things about them.

CHAPTER 1: HOMES IN THE FORESTS

Native Americans look to nature for a place to live and for building materials. They use trees, plants, stone, mud, clay, sod, and animal hides to make their homes. They use what they find in the areas where they live. There has always been a strong relationship between Native Americans and the environment.

Geography and climate determine how homes are built and what materials are used. In the vast forests of the Northeast, trees and bark or grass mats give shelter. In the desert Southwest, there are few trees, so homes are made of adobe. Cedar trees abound in the Northwest, so houses are made of cedar planking that is decorated with beautiful carvings.

Look at the area you live in now. How do you think you would build your house?

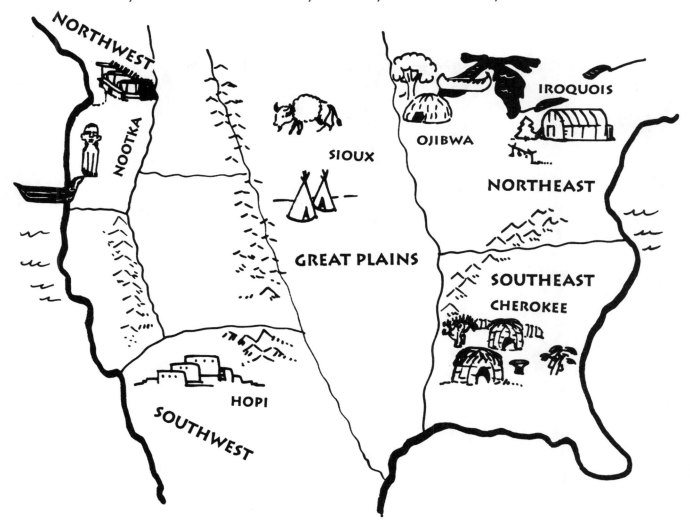

Teacher: *Story Cards* on pages 7 through 9 should be presented to your groups when they begin work on a specific Native American tribe in this chapter. Reproduce one *Story Card* for each group.

Social Skills: Work toward a goal, summarize, elaborate.
Academic Skill: Understand and list general requirements for wilderness living.
Teacher: Reproduce one Word Web for each group.

LIVING IN THE FORESTS

What things would you need to live in the woods with your family? Take turns writing the items on the cedar tree trunks.

Word Web

DANCING SQUIRREL (ALGONQUIAN)

My name is Dancing Squirrel. I am an Ojibwa in the Algonquian nation. My family and I live together in our wigwam in a vast birch forest. We do not live near other families except during special events. The trees are very big here and evenly spaced. We leave most of the trees standing because they are very hard to cut down.

We hunt animals for most of our food, so we move often to stay near wild game. Whenever we move, we have to build a new wigwam to shelter our family from the weather. To build our wigwam, my father and I make the frame from 16 to 20 poles cut from long saplings. We stick them firmly in the ground in a circle and strap the ends together with cedar bark. My mother and grandmother finish the wigwam. Men only cut the saplings and build the frame. The rest is women's work.

My mother and grandmother cover the frame with large mats made of cattail rushes. In winter they use slabs of elm bark. The roof is made of birch bark. A smoke hole is left in the center to let the smoke from our fire out.

GOLDEN FAWN (IROQUOIS)

I am Golden Fawn. I am an Oneida of the Iroquois Nation. My family and I live in a village of longhouses surrounded by a stockade. We live in the village most of the year except when the men hunt deer or the women go nutting. Our farm fields are outside the stockade.

My family and our dog live with seven other families in our longhouse. It has a frame of tall elm poles on the sides and two rows of taller poles running down the center inside the house. The rafters are bent into arches joined by long purlins (horizontal supporting timbers). The walls and roof are completly covered with elm bark. The bark is held in place by more poles. There are only two doors in either end and no windows.

Inside the house is one huge room divided by bark partitions. Each family has a large bunk covered with skins and a storage cell. Above the bunk is a shelf where my brother and I sleep. We also store things there.

There are cooking fires all down the center of the house. We share a fire with our neighbors across from us. There is no hole in the roof, and the house is always very smoky.

WHITE CLAY (CHEROKEE)

My parents call me White Clay. We are of the Cherokee tribe in the Iroquois nation. We live in the southeast mountains. Our winter home is made of large wooden posts set in the ground. We mix grass with smooth clay to cover the posts to make walls. The roof is covered with bark and thatch made of thick grass. My mother cooks our food in a fireplace at the center of the room. Smoke goes out a hole in the roof. Our beds are raised off the floor on posts. They are covered with hemlock boughs and woven mats. The winter house is small and warm. The summer house is open and airy. We entertain our visitors there. The remaining buildings are for storage of food, tools, and things we trade to other villages.

In the center of town is a square where the ceremonial buildings are. The *uku*, our chief, also has his house there. The huge council house has seven sides. Many of our ceremonies are held here. Outside the council house is a huge yard where we play games, dance and have ceremonies on special days. Our crops are planted outside of town.

TALL GRASS WAVING (SIOUX)

I am Tall Grass Waving. My people, the Sioux, hunt buffalo. We follow the herds over grassy plains where there are few trees. We live in a tipi. It is a conical tent that is warm in winter and cool in summer. Every spring my mother and her friends sew twenty or thirty hides together to make a new tipi cover. We have a big feast to make the sewing more fun. She decorates the inside and my father decorates the outside with pictures of his powers or his bravery in the hunt. When the tribal council is held in early summer, there are scores of gleaming new white tipis glowing like lanterns at night. By the following spring, the tops are black with smoke and the bottom edges are brown.

We sleep on grass pallets covered with hides. The beds on the left are for our family. The beds on the right are saved for guests. The fire is toward the back of the tipi, where smoke flows out through a hole at the top. Working together our family can put up or take down our tipi in three minutes. We have to pack quickly to be able to move fast when the buffalo are sighted.

RAIN IN HER HAIR (HOPI PUEBLO)

Our pueblo ("small town" in Spanish) is high on a mesa above the Painted Desert. In the center of town is a ceremonial dance court and *kivas*. My father is *kiva* chief. He is responsible for the underground temple where men and boys go to weave, to talk, and to prepare for ceremonies. My mother and I go into the *kiva* only on very special days to watch the men perform ceremonies.

My family lives in a home called a pueblo. Father built the foundation and hauled timbers from the valley below. My mother and I built the rest. We used stones, mud, and adobe to make the walls. There are few windows and the door is in the roof. We climb down into the house on a ladder. There is one big room where we sleep, prepare meals, and visit with friends. The fireplace in the corner is for cooking. The chimney is made of old clay pots with the bottoms broken out. We stack them up over the fireplace to guide the smoke's flow through the roof. We burn coal because wood is very scarce here. The pole suspended from the ceiling is for hanging our clothes and blankets when we don't need them. A small back room is for storing corn, our most important food.

RAVEN'S BEAK (NOOTKA)

Our village of cedar plank houses sits on the edge of the ocean with forested mountains in the background. There is a tall carved effigy pole that shows the animal my family represents. My family owns this house where several other related families live. Each family has its own fireplace and low plank beds covered with cedar mats and furs. Above the rafters of the house hangs smoked salmon which is our favorite food. The roof boards at the center of the house can be removed to let the smoke out of the house. There are no windows in the house, but we get light from the fires and from dried candlefish. These fish are so oily, that with a cedar bark wick, they will burn for a long time, like a candle.

We do no farming. We hunt, fish and gather plants for our food. Because we don't have to spend so much time working, we have time to do other things, like wood carving. We decorate everything we own, from our homes to our elaborate ceremonial costumes.

Social Skills: Seek accuracy, integrate a number of ideas, work together.
Academic Skill: Follow directions, recognize materials and complete the wigwam.
Teacher: Reproduce a *Story Card* and *Role Card* for each group. Help gather materials for each group.

BUILDING AN ALGONQUIAN WIGWAM

Read about Dancing Squirrel's home. Work together to make a small wigwam. Gather materials and follow the directions on your role card to construct it.

Role Cards

Teammates 1 and 2: (boys)

Materials:
Shallow cardboard box or lid
Sand or dirt
16-20 10" bendable twigs (willow works well)
string or narrow masking tape
Directions:
1. Fill box or lid with slightly damp sand.
2. Stick 12 twigs in a circle into the sand.
3. Bring twigs together at the top and tie or tape into a dome shape.
4. Tie or tape remaining twigs around the dome to complete the frame.

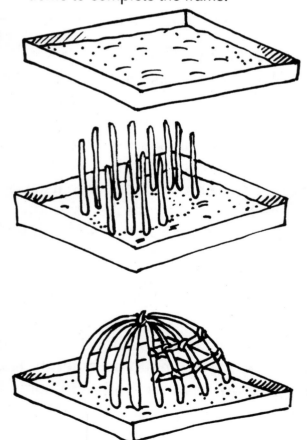

Teammates 3 and 4: (girls)

Materials:
Brown paper grocery bags
Pieces of birch bark or white paper
glue
Directions:
1. Tear paper bags into small rectangles about 2" x 4".
2. Glue them to the frame, overlapping the edges. Start at the bottom and work up.
3. Leave an area open on one side for the door.
4. Glue the birch bark or pieces of white paper over the top of the frame for the roof. Leave a small section at the top of the dome for the smoke hole.

Social Skills: Use praise words, no put-downs, participate, elaborate.
Academic Skill: Identify and draw the elements needed to create a typical Iroquois village.
Teacher: Reproduce one *Story Card* and one *Illustration Sheet* for each group.

AN IROQUOIS VILLAGE

While one person reads Golden Fawn's story, listen and take notes about the village. Create a poster showing Golden Fawn's village. Talk together about what to include and where it should be. This illustration sheet will help you draw and color what you need.

Iroquois Village Illustration Sheet

longhouse

stockade

hunter

drying fish

preparing hides

making moccasins

Social Skills: Use quiet voices, participate, integrate ideas.
Academic Skill: Identify village areas, create buildings and put them on the bulletin board.
Teacher: Group children according to their choice of Summer House, Winter House, Crops, and Council House. Reproduce one *Story Card* and *Worksheet* for each group. Bring all the elements from each group together and arrange them on a bulletin board.

WHITE CLAY'S CHEROKEE VILLAGE

Read about White Clay's village. Work with your teammates to create your section of the village. Use the pictures and the story to help you create an entire village on a bulletin board. Draw pieces larger, if necessary, to fit on your bulletin board.

Cherokee Village Worksheets

Cherokee Summer House Worksheet

inside   outside

Cherokee Winter House Worksheet

inside   outside

Cherokee Council House Worksheet

seven-sided council house

nearby yard for games and ceremonies

Cherokee Corn Worksheet

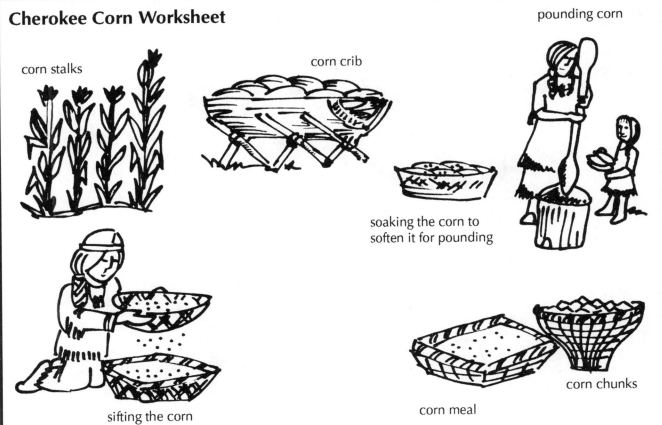

pounding corn

corn stalks

corn crib

soaking the corn to
soften it for pounding

sifting the corn

corn meal

corn chunks

Social Skills: Integrate ideas into one, work toward a goal, use quiet voices.
Academic Skill: Follow directions to make a tipi.
Teacher: Reproduce one sheet for each group. Help gather materials. If several groups are participating, display all the tipis together for a Tribal Council/Buffalo Hunt. Younger children may want to decorate the tipi and omit the skin-pasting portion.

MAKE A TABLE TOP TIPI

Read Tall Grass Waving's story. Work together to make one tipi. Take turns following each step. The cutting and pasting activities let you pretend to make a real tipi from buffalo skins.

Materials:

two tipi patterns
scissors
glue
markers or crayons
wooden skewers

To Make:

1. Cut out the tipi skin pieces on the dotted lines from one pattern.
2. Glue the pieces onto the second pattern in the proper places.
3. Decorate the outside of the tipi with hunting designs.
4. Decorate the inside of the tipi with sun and cloud designs. Fold back flaps on dotted lines.
5. Glue wooden skewers to the inside of the tipi on the heavy black lines. Allow to dry completely.
6. Put glue on the dot. Paste tipi together as shown.

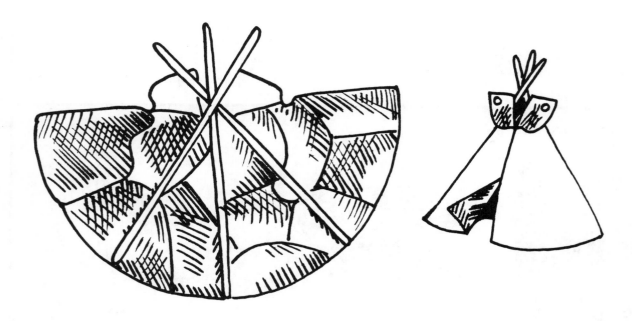

Sun and Cloud Designs

Hunting Designs

14

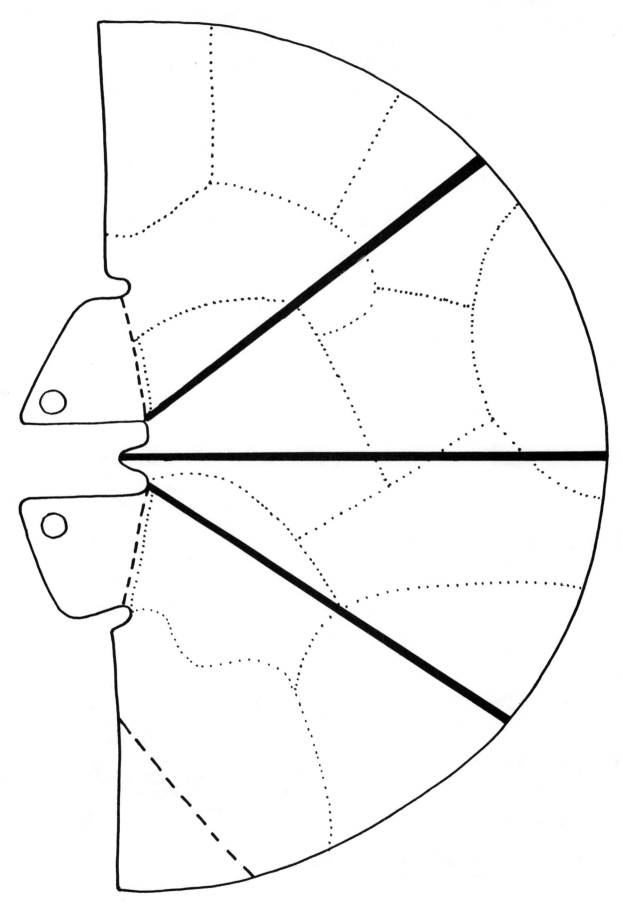

Social Skill: Stay in group, no put-downs, seek accuracy.
Academic Skill: Identify and recreate Hopi buildings
Teacher: Reproduce *Story Card*, directions and *Furnishings* for each group. When completed, stack houses on a table to simulate a Hopi village.

A HOPI PUEBLO HOUSE

Read about Rain in Her Hair's home. Use white gift boxes to construct a pueblo house.

Materials:
1 square gift box with lid
scissors
glue
markers or crayons
Hopi Pueblo furnishings
twigs or cardboard for ladder

To Make:
1. Cut a square hole in the box lid for the door.
2. Stick the wooden skewer in box bottom as shown.
3. Color and cut out the house furnishings. Glue inside box as shown in diagram. Put the box cover back in place.
4. Make a ladder of wooden twigs or cut from cardboard.
5. A number of boxes can be placed side by side and stacked to create a Pueblo village.

Assembly Diagrams:

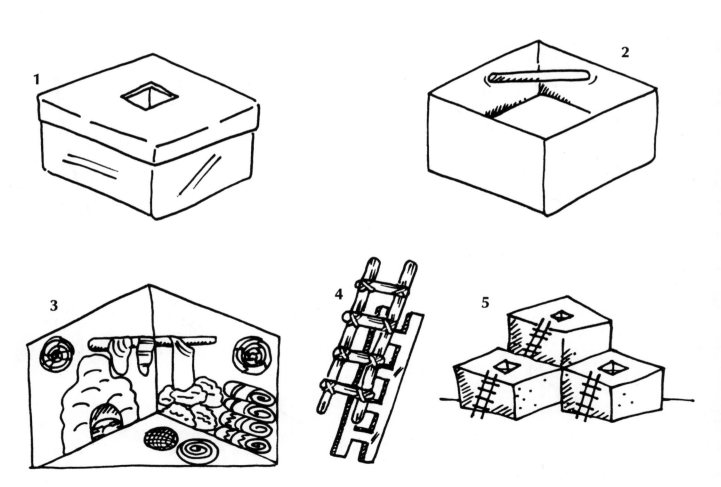

Hopi Pueblo Furnishings

clay pot fireplace

stacks of corn (black, white, red, yellow, and blue)

clothing to hang on the stick

baskets (hang on walls and put on floor)

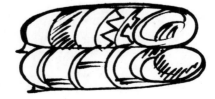

blankets

Social Skills: Participate, work toward a goal, ask for help.
Academic Skill: Understand how a Nootka village was organized.
Teacher: Reproduce one page of *Stick-ems* and a *Nootka Village Scene* for each group. Team members each get Stick-em pieces to color and cut out. The *Nootka Village Scene* is passed around. Members place stickers where they fit best.

BUILD A NOOTKA VILLAGE

Read about Raven's Beak's home. Work together to color and cut out the stick-em pieces. Pass the scene around for each member to add stick-ems where they fit in the scene.

Village Stick-ems

whaling canoes

plank houses (place along shore)

cooking box

whaling equipment (put under house)

cedar trees

secret shrine with carved effigies

Social Skills: Speak clearly, listen actively, participate.
Academic Skills: Understand and tell how Native American homes are different for each tribe in this chapter.
Teacher: Get question lists from each group. As a group is called, they stand together. Call out a number and ask a question. The person with that number answers the question for the group.

TELL US WHAT YOU'VE LEARNED

Team members choose one tribe that they have studied. The team makes a list of questions about the houses they live in and their environment. Discuss the answers so that every member of the team knows every answer.

Question Sheet

NATIVE AMERICAN HOMES QUESTIONS

Our Tribe Name: _____

Questions About Homes and Environment:

_____

_____

_____

_____

_____

_____

_____

_____

_____

_____

_____

_____

_____

_____

_____

CHAPTER 2: HOW DO NATIVE AMERICANS DRESS?

Native Americans learn when very young how to use their abundant resources and crafting skills to create a wide variety of decorative, comfortable clothing and body coverings. The wild plants that grow nearby, such as bullrushes, grasses, corn husks, and elm or cedar bark, are prepared to make the fibers that are woven, looped, knitted, braided, or twined into sandals, clothing, or blankets. Other plants are used to make the dyes that color the fibers to make the garments pleasing to see and wear. Many tribes have special colors and patterns they use to show their talents. The colors and patterns used by each tribe are more then just decoration; they are used to tell the tribal stories and histories, too. Colors are very important as face and body paints used in religious ceremonies, storytelling, and everyday beautifying!

Wild animals such as deer, elk, antelope, and buffalo provide skin and hair to be used for buckskin shoes, wallets, leggings, and dresses. All the tribes except the Nootka in the Northwest have some type of moccasin pattern and no matter what the style, they fit each foot perfectly and are comfortable. They are often beautifully beaded or painted in intricate designs. In this chapter you will learn some traditional techniques as well as simple classroom adaptations to create Native American clothing to wear or use for Indian characters and displays. Take the time and effort to make your designs useful, comfortable, and decorative, something you and your group members will be proud to show!

Teacher: Read the above information to young students or record on cassette for groups to listen. Reproduce for groups of readers to use.

21

Social Skills: No put-downs, work toward a goal, integrate ideas.
Academic Skills: Create authentic costumes for tribal families and extend the knowledge of creating other fashions.
Teacher: Have each group choose a tribe to represent. Reproduce a set of *Dressing Up Characters*, *Clothing Patterns*, *Tribe Cards,* and *Add-Ons* for each group. Have medium-weight tagboard on hand to mount characters for display. Each member will choose and assemble the appropriate materials to decorate and dress one family member (girl, boy, mother, father) of a tribe.

DRESSING UP

Each member of your group creates a different Native American character to complete your tribal family.

Dressing Up Characters

Mother

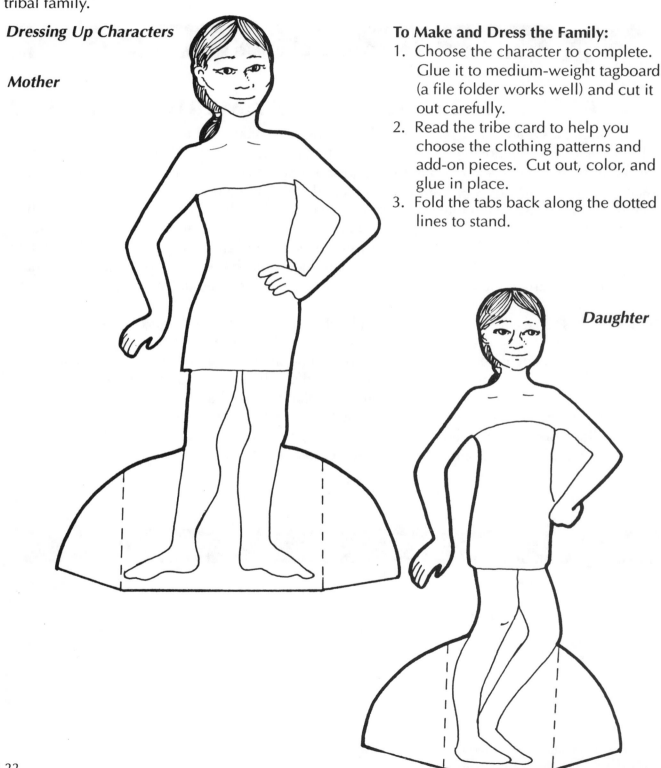

Daughter

To Make and Dress the Family:
1. Choose the character to complete. Glue it to medium-weight tagboard (a file folder works well) and cut it out carefully.
2. Read the tribe card to help you choose the clothing patterns and add-on pieces. Cut out, color, and glue in place.
3. Fold the tabs back along the dotted lines to stand.

More Dressing Up Characters
Use these characters with the Dressing Up activity.

Son

Father

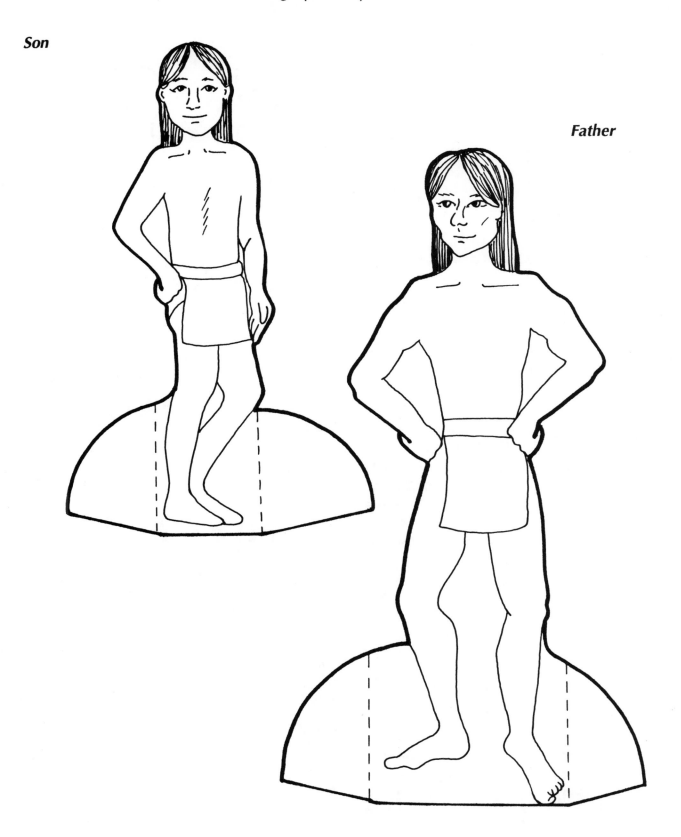

Dressing Up Clothing Patterns

Decorate, color, and cut out these patterns to use with the tribe cards and add-ons to dress your Native American family. Cut fringes in the edges for a fancier look!

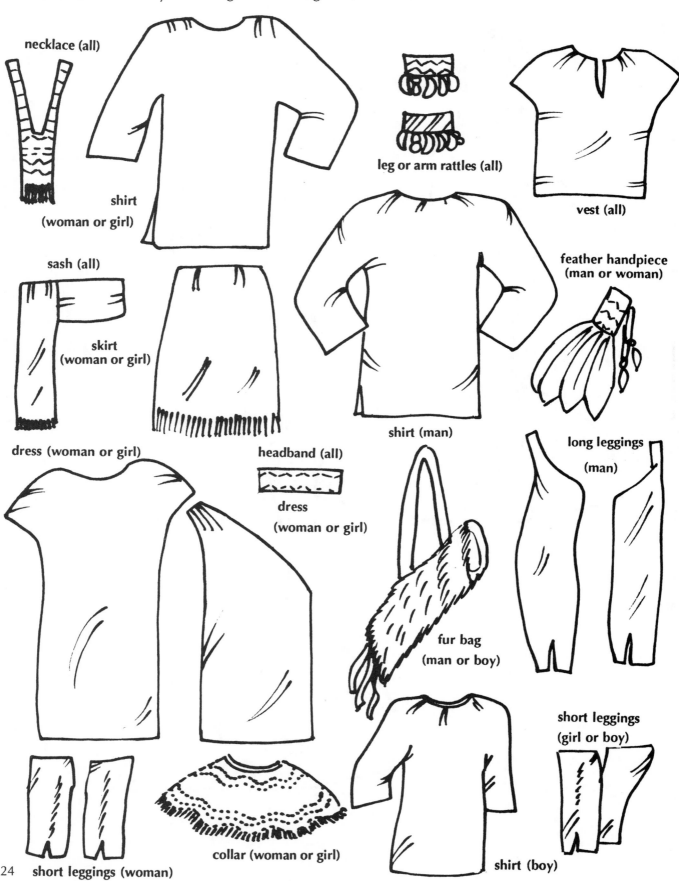

necklace (all)

shirt
(woman or girl)

leg or arm rattles (all)

vest (all)

sash (all)

skirt
(woman or girl)

feather handpiece
(man or woman)

shirt (man)

dress (woman or girl)

headband (all)

dress
(woman or girl)

long leggings
(man)

fur bag
(man or boy)

short leggings
(girl or boy)

collar (woman or girl)

shirt (boy)

short leggings (woman)

Dressing Up Tribe Cards:
Read the cards to find out how to dress your characters with the clothing patterns and add-ons.

TRIBE CARD 1. DANCING SQUIRREL (OJIBWA)

Our people dress in deerskin clothing. Very little sewing is involved. Sewing animal skins is very difficult with only stone or bone tools. Everyone wears moccasins most of the time, and we decorate them with beautiful floral designs. My father wears a warm fur turban in the winter. My mother makes lacy beaded collars to wear over her dress, and decorative sashes for us all.

Ojibwa Add-Ons Color, cut out, and paste on the characters to dress your Ojibwa person.

decorative sash

embroidered collar

moccasins

fur turban

TRIBE CARD 2. GOLDEN FAWN (IROQUOIS)

The tribe dresses in deerskin much like Dancing Squirrel. Our people are more fond of fringe on our clothing than the Ojibwa. In winter the women wear a fringed cape with two arm slits. Women wear their hair in a single braid or loose ponytail. Men wear kilts over their leggings and carry a tobacco pouch over one shoulder. *Sachems* (chiefs) and shamans wear their hair loose. Warriors shave their heads, wear it in a fringe on top with one feather.

Iroquois Add-Ons Color, cut out, and paste on the characters to dress your Iroquois person.

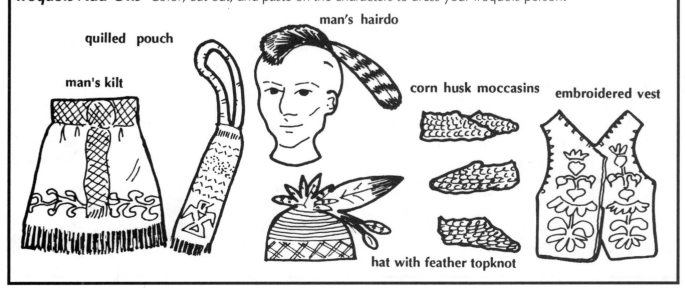

quilled pouch

man's hairdo

man's kilt

corn husk moccasins

embroidered vest

hat with feather topknot

Dressing Up Tribe Cards:
Read the cards to find out how to dress your characters with the clothing patterns and add-ons.

TRIBE CARD 3. WHITE CLAY (CHEROKEE)

My family and I dress very simply. In summer the men wear just a loincloth and go barefoot. My mother wears a only a skirt, adding a robe on colder days. We enjoy decorating our bodies with paints in dots and stripes. Our costumes are simple, but we wear necklaces made of shells, beads, and animal teeth. We carry decorative fringed bags for hunting or gathering food. Men wear their hair long and loose with a headband or a single feather in their hair. Our chief wears a cloak of wild turkey feathers and a feather headdress.

Cherokee Add-Ons Color, cut out, and paste on the character to dress your Cherokee person.

leather sash

feathered headdress

fringed bag

beaver tooth necklace

TRIBE CARD 4. RAIN IN HER HAIR (HOPI)

The Hopi Indians are very peaceful farmers. We do not fight in wars unless we are attacked first. People say we are good-humored and clever traders and craftsmen. I wear my hair in the "squash blossom" buns on either side of my head. Mother wore the same buns before she married. Now she wears two pendants representing squash fruits. We both wear blue cotton dresses, dyed with sunflower seeds. Dresses are rectangular sheets joined at the corners over the right shoulder. The colorful narrow sash is wrapped around the waist several times.

Men and boys wear white kilts and brightly colored sashes around the waist. On special days an animal pelt hangs from the back. Men wear headbands over their cropped hair. Both men and women wear tall white moccasins and bead and stone necklaces. In cool weather cotton blankets are worn over the shoulders. Young children dress like their parents or go nude until they are about nine.

Hopi Add-Ons Color, cut out, and paste on the character to dress your Hopi Native American.

woman's moccasins **turquoise jewelry** **headband** **girl's hairdo** **woman's hairdo**

Dressing Up Tribe Cards:
Read the cards to find out how to dress your characters with the clothing patterns and add-ons.

TRIBE CARD 5. TALL GRASS WAVING (SIOUX)

We use the buffalo to make almost everything we need. Buffalo robes are very heavy, so we prefer deer or elk skins for our clothing. We decorate our shirts, dresses, and skirts with paints, feathers, porcupine quills, and beads. Often we draw scenes from our lives or travels. Other symbols are sacred and used for special ceremonies. Eagle feathers are very important to warriors. A man is given an eagle feather every time he performs a daring feat. A man with a very long war bonnet is a man to be respected. He has collected so many feathers for brave or wise deeds that his war bonnet touches the ground. Single feathers are worn every day. A feather headdress known as our "war bonnet" is for special ceremonies and for riding into war. It is big medicine. It protects the warrior in battle.

Sioux Add-Ons   Color, cut out, and paste on the character to dress your Sioux Native American.

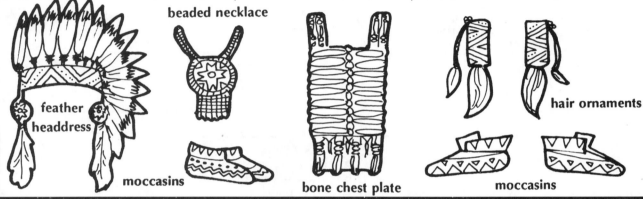

beaded necklace

feather headdress

moccasins

bone chest plate

hair ornaments

moccasins

TRIBE CARD 6. RAVEN'S BEAK (NOOTKA)

I live in the Northwest, where it rains a lot. I wear clothing to stay dry. It's never very cold here. Most of our clothing is made of woven cedar bark, like my cape and rain hat. There are huge cedar trees everywhere and we use them for almost everything we make. At ceremonies my father wears a sea otter fur robe. We wear colorful fringed Chilkat shirts which are often given away at our rituals called potlatches. Everyone goes barefoot most of the time.

Nootka Add-Ons   Color, cut out, and paste on the character to dress your Nootka person.

cedar mat cape   chilkat shirt

woven rain hat

Extending Activity: NATIVE AMERICAN FASHION SHOW Team Share
Have each team member prepare a written description of his or her costume on a small note card. These can be displayed in your classroom or read "fashion show" style as groups show each other their completed characters in costume.

NATIVE AMERICAN MAKEUP

Native American men paint their faces to please unseen spirits and to ask for their help, to frighten evil spirits and enemies, to please and impress their tribe or to please themselves! Face and body painting is seen as a means of obtaining magic. The colors and symbols make them look and feel powerful. Earthen paints are finely ground and mixed with sunflower oil, nut oil, or animal fat to make face paint: Earthy clays like ochre contain iron oxide and are mixed to make red or yellow paints. White comes from kaolin clay, gypsum (rocks containing calcium), and limestone. Black is made from powdered charcoal and coal. Paints are considered "magic" and are kept reverently in a special bag. Some tribes sing songs over the paint to protect it from harmful influence. Different face paint colors mean these different things to different tribes:

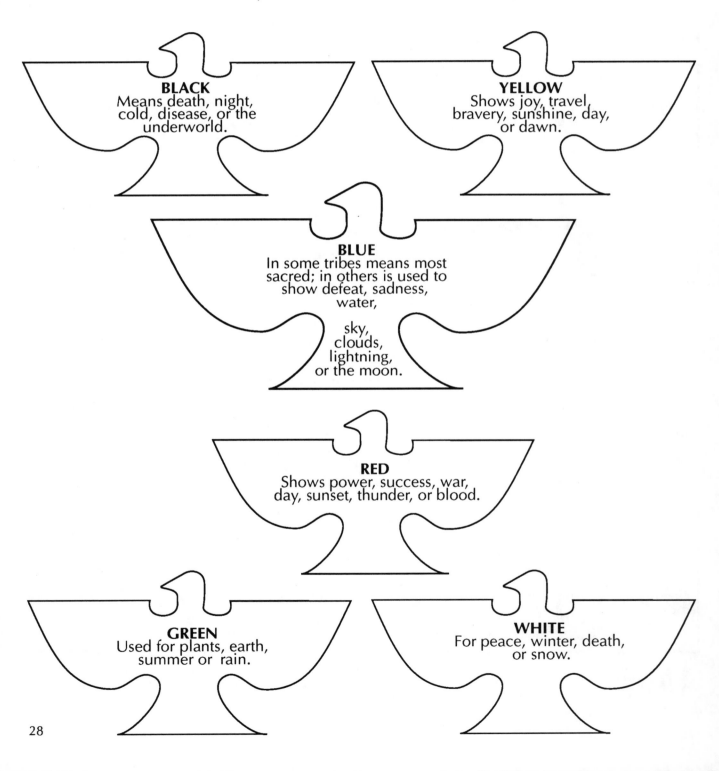

BLACK
Means death, night, cold, disease, or the underworld.

YELLOW
Shows joy, travel, bravery, sunshine, day, or dawn.

BLUE
In some tribes means most sacred; in others is used to show defeat, sadness, water,

sky, clouds, lightning, or the moon.

RED
Shows power, success, war, day, sunset, thunder, or blood.

GREEN
Used for plants, earth, summer or rain.

WHITE
For peace, winter, death, or snow.

Iroquois Men use different paints to become the characters in their dances:

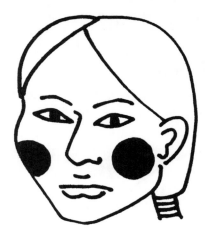

Great Sky Eagle Dance
(red spot on each cheek)

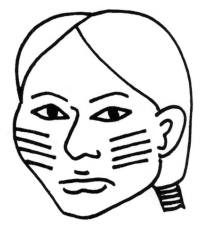

War Dancers
(four stripes of red on each cheek)

Bear Dance
(paint right cheek black)

Thunder God Dance
(four lightning streaks radiating
from eyes and running down cheeks,
or lines in groups of four upon the
forehead, cheeks, and chin)

Northwest peoples paint animals such as the thunderbird, otter, wolf, or eagle on their bodies. Sometimes the designs are tattooed into the skin.

Hopi peoples have special makeup (as well as masks) to represent religious figures called Kachinas. They have as many as 250 different patterns representing good spirits, animals, birds, clowns, and mudhead characters.

Native American women use face paints, too, but for different reasons. In the Iroquois tribe, you are considered beautiful when you wear red-colored powder all over your face. This is where the term *redskins* came from. Women enjoy painting each other's faces because mirrors are not available. Their designs are often part of individual religious ceremonies, but favorite designs are round dots, lines, and large red spots on the cheeks or forehead. They do not usually use animal designs. Sometimes they even paint the part in their hair red or yellow. The only time black paint is used is when a family member has died.

Social Skills: Listen actively, seek accuracy, ask for help when needed.
Academic Skills: Create a face design using natural colors.
Teacher: Reproduce a *Face Paint Pattern* for each partner. Have pairs use the introduction material as a guide to designing tribal face paint patterns. Have them each do a design on the blank face shown, then discuss together what the designs mean and how they will be used.

FACE PAINT PATTERNS

Use colors and designs to create a special face paint pattern. Think about what the colors and symbols will mean, talk about it with your partner, and write it below:

Face to Paint

Colors Used	Meaning	Symbols Used	Meaning

Extending Activity 1: FACE PAINT PUT-ONS Turn to your Partner
Use nontoxic face paints to follow your colored patterns. Decorate your partner's face.

Extending Activity 2: TELL-A-MYTH Stand and Share
Learn a Native American myth or legend provided on page 77. Create face paint designs for the characters and perform for your groups.

Social Skills: Quiet voices, ask for help, positive.
Academic Skills: Make and fit authentic designs of Native American clothing. Embellish with appropriate motifs.
Teacher: These are smaller versions of actual moccasin patterns, which will work nicely for displays or bulletin boards. Reproduce one *Mini Moccasin Pattern* for each group to use. Each group member will complete one step in the process, then pass the moccasin on to the next member.

MINI MOCCASINS

Work together to cut out, stitch, and decorate each moccasin. Decide who will do each step, then pass the moccasin around to each member to do their part until it is finished.

Materials (for both moccasins):	**Stitching Patterns (choose one):**
pencil, sharp scissors, thin cotton felt, heavy thread or yarn, darning needle 8" thin leather or yarn laces (Plains) Glass seed beads, beading thread, and needles Red, black, green, blue fabric markers	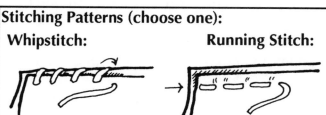

Woodland Stocking Moccasin Pattern

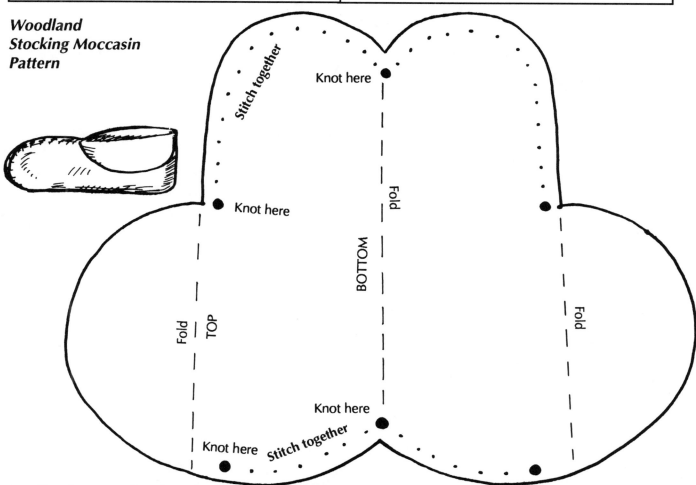

Woodland Moccasin Directions:

1. Cut out the pattern and trace it onto felt. (Both right and left shoes are the same.) Cut out the felt along outer edges. Fold moccasin up at center.
2. Use a whipstitch or running stitch (see diagrams) to sew the moccasin sides together along the outer edge from toe to the middle of the top.
3. Sew along the heel. Knot the sewing securely at both ends. Fold down the rounded flaps at the top.
4. Use beads or fabric markers to decorate your moccasins. Use the design ideas on pages 33 and 34 to indicate a special tribe or area.

Plains Low Moccasin

Plains Moccasin Directions:

1. Cut out the pattern and trace two onto felt. Flip the pattern over after the first one is traced to give you a right and left shoe. Cut slits carefully.
2. Use a whipstitch or running stitch (see diagram on page 31) to sew the moccasin top to the bottom along the outer edge from the front along the side to the back.
3. Fold flaps at the back over as shown to form the heel. Stitch through all the flaps in an X to secure. Cut small slits around the top edge of the shoe and thread the strip of leather through.
4. Use beads or fabric markers to decorate your moccasins. Use the design ideas on pages 33 and 34 to indicate a special tribe or area.

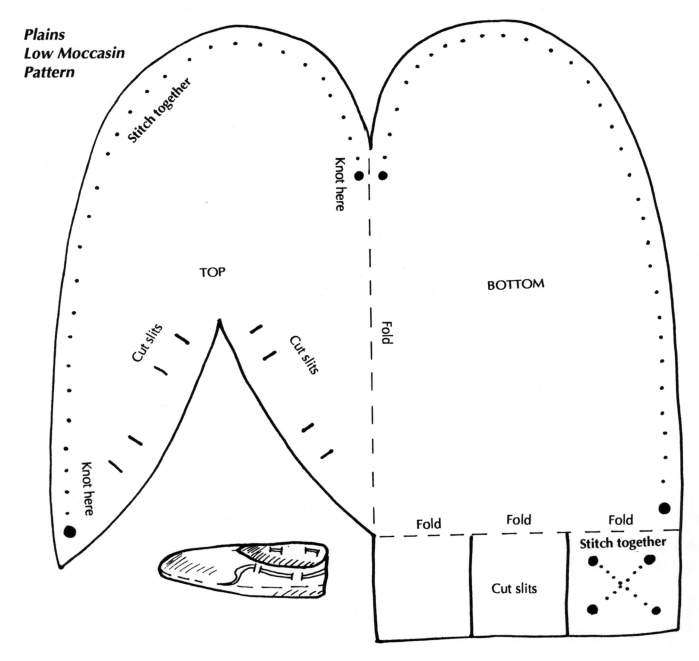

Plains Low Moccasin Pattern

Stitch together

Knot here

TOP

BOTTOM

Fold

Cut slits

Cut slits

Knot here

Fold   Fold   Fold

Stitch together

Cut slits

 Extending Activity: FIT-A-MOCCASIN for Partners
Enlarge the patterns given. Create fullsize fashions. Partners help each other trace and fit the patterns to their feet. Adapt design patterns to make original styles!

Social Skills: Elaborate, participate, extend another's answers.
Academic Skills: Recognize symbols used and elaborate to create more.
Teacher: Feature a different tribal group in each area of the classroom. Children go to their area of interest. Reproduce a *Native American Design Ideas* section for each group member to use in developing designs for mini moccasins and wearable crafts. Children work as a group, passing the papers around to add a new design to each.

NATIVE AMERICAN DESIGN IDEAS

Use these descriptions to develop your own designs to decorate moccasins, arm bands, leg bands, and other Native American crafts.

PLAINS (SIOUX) DESIGNS
Triangles and other geometric shapes are combined in many ways.

Practice drawing your own Plains designs here:

WOODLAND (ALGONQUIAN AND IROQUOIS) DESIGNS
Flowers, plant shapes, animals, and thin double-curving lines are used for decoration.

Practice drawing your own Woodland designs here:

SOUTHWEST (HOPI) DESIGNS

Animals and nature shapes, cactus, corn, clouds, mountains, and suns are also popular.

Practice drawing your own Southwest designs here:

NORTHWEST COAST (NOOTKA) DESIGNS

Animals and people are shown with thick curved lines.

Practice drawing your own Northwest designs here:

Social Skills: Form groups quietly, participate, ask for help.
Academic Skills: Follow steps to re-create Native American wearable crafts.
Teacher: Students go to their area of interest, then pair up to learn and complete the crafts. The materials lists below will help you get ready. Save these wearable crafts to use and wear later in the celebrations described in chapter 5.

NATIVE AMERICAN DECORATIVE CRAFTS

Sioux Mock Porcupine Quill Hair Ornament/Arm Band Materials List

- quilling facts and tips page 37
- 1 thin paper plate per student
- pencil (1 per student)
- hair ornament/arm band pattern page 38
- 1(1 lb.) bag of raffia (comes in assorted colors in arts/crafts stores)
- darning needle or raffia needle
- scissors
- heavy brown paper or tagboard
- thick cord
- feathers (optional; find bagged in craft stores)

Iroquois Mock Beaded Pocket Bag Materials List

- bag pattern suggestions from page 39
- white and brown paper for patterns
- scissors
- crayons or colored pencils
- white glue (or stitch together—stitches shown on page 31)
- Red, blue, yellow, and black acrylic fabric paints (shiny kind in small bottles)
- paper punch
- yarn (to make ties and stitch together)
- feathers and pony beads to decorate ties (optional)

Southwest Bow-Loom Co-Op Sashes Materials List

- co-op sash directions on page 40
- sturdy green branch or bough about 20"–24" in length (1 per study group)
- 6" thin sticks (2 per loom)
- sturdy string
- 3 or 4 yarn colors (3–5 sashes per skein, depending on how tightly it's woven)
- scissors

Iroquois Leg Rattles and False Face Mask Materials List

- leg rattle pattern from page 41
- mask pattern from page 42
- cardboard tubes or oatmeal boxes (Cut into sections, each box makes 2–4 rattles)
- tagboard (face mask or rattles)
- white glue
- scissors
- red, brown, yellow, and black markers or paints (don't use paint that flakes off)
- raffia, corn husks, or yarn for fringe
- yarn for ties
- shells, beads, shell buttons (to make rattles; bells optional)
- metallic permanent marker (optional)

Plains Feather and Bead Chest Plate Materials List

- bead, feather preparation how-to's on page 43
  Note: See handmade bead recipe on page 43 for additional materials.
- chest plate pattern on page 44
- tagboard or corrugated cardboard
- paper punch
- heavy cotton or leather cord (6"–12" lengths per chest plate)
- shells (with holes for stringing)
- plastic straws (4 per chest plate, cut in half)
- handmade beads (or substitute purchased wooden or large glass beads)
- small feathers (optional)

Mock Southwest Silver Pendant and Belt Buckle Materials List

- jewelry patterns from page 45
- heavyweight aluminum foil
- corrugated cardboard or heavy tagboard
- tool for "metalwork" (pencil, cuticle stick, sharp rock, shell)
- paper punch and cord for pendant string
- tape (if needed to attach belt buckle)

Northwest Bear Mask Materials List:

- mask pattern page 46
- tagboard or cardboard (for pattern base)
- scissors
- yellow, blue, and green yarn (plenty, for heavy yarn coverage)
- white tacky glue (plenty!)

Sioux Warrior Headdress Materials List:

- headband and feather patterns pages 47–49
- tagboard
- construction paper
- scissors
- crayons or markers
- glue
- yarn for ties (two 18" lengths per headdress)

Extending activity: ARTISTS IN RESIDENCE Team Share
The members of each craft group take their projects to other groups to show and explain about them. When all the groups have had a chance to share, sign up for another craft day when you will be trying another project.

Teacher: Have students practice these quilling techniques and patterns before making the hair ornament or arm band craft. **Note:** We suggest using raffia to replace the porcupine quills which would not be available to most classrooms; however the stitching techniques are taken from original designs.

PORCUPINE QUILLING FACTS AND TIPS

Porcupine quilling is a unique, original Native American craft. Women take quills from the porcupine, cut off the sharp, barbed tips (ouch!) wash, dye, and soak the quills to make them soft. Then they pull the damp quills through their teeth to make them flat. Each quill is wrapped or folded and sewn onto thread or skins. Sometimes quills are sewn into birchbark to decorate baskets. It is a very slow process, but many tribes take pride in making the colorful precise designs. Iroquois Peoples make designs with curved lines of quilling sewn onto vests, leggings, and bags. Algonquian tribes create round sewing baskets covered with naturalistic animals or flowers. Sometimes the whole basket is covered. Plains peoples use simple, bold shapes and wrapped, folded, and braided quills to cover buckskin, peace pipes, bags, and belts. Northwest tribes wrap quills on the fringe of costumes or sew them on in bold animal designs.

Quilling Techniques:

Practice working with 6" lengths of raffia and needles to create these designs. Glue the pattern below to a thin paper plate, your "birchbark" base. Use a pencil to punch the dots, then stitch and wrap the raffia as shown. When you feel comfortable with the craft of quilling, try the quilling project on page 38.

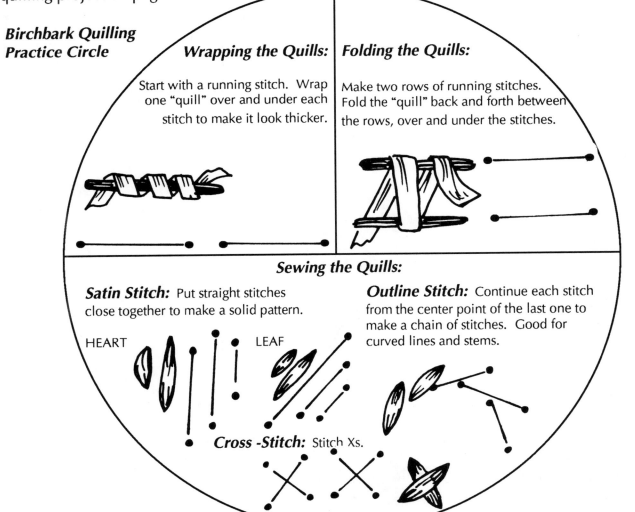

Birchbark Quilling Practice Circle

Wrapping the Quills: Start with a running stitch. Wrap one "quill" over and under each stitch to make it look thicker.

Folding the Quills: Make two rows of running stitches. Fold the "quill" back and forth between the rows, over and under the stitches.

Sewing the Quills:

Satin Stitch: Put straight stitches close together to make a solid pattern.

HEART   LEAF

Outline Stitch: Continue each stitch from the center point of the last one to make a chain of stitches. Good for curved lines and stems.

Cross -Stitch: Stitch Xs.

Social Skills: Positive support, vocalization, participation.
Academic Skills: Follow steps to re-create Native American wearable crafts.
Teacher: Reproduce a *Hair Ornament/Arm Band Pattern* on heavy brown paper or tagboard for each student. Make sure they have read and practiced the quilling techniques on page 37.

SIOUX MOCK PORCUPINE QUILL
HAIR ORNAMENT AND ARM BAND

Pairs Check Directions:

1. Cut out the band.
2. Use the quilling stitches you learned on page 37 to add colorful designs to the band. Create your own ideas using the guide below:

satin stitch: wrapping: cross-stitch:

3. When stitching is complete, cut a 12" length of yarn and center it on the top. Fold the flap over the yarn and glue it in place.
4. Add more yarn or raffia fringe to the bottom of the strip, as well as longer lengths tied with feathers or beads for decoration.
5. Hang from top end on braid or barrette to wear as a hairpiece. Punch bottom holes and wrap around arm and tie to wear as an arm band.

Hair Ornament/Arm Band Pattern

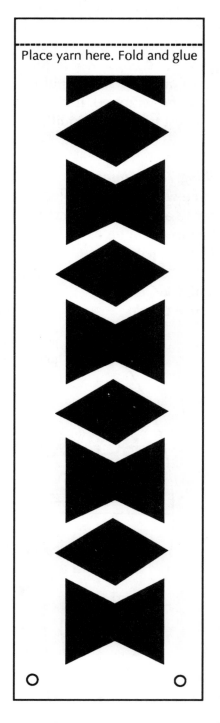

Place yarn here. Fold and glue

Note: The same pattern is used for both. Hang long with feathered cords for hair. Wrap band around arm and tie cords for arm band.

38

Social Skills: Positive support, vocalization, participate.
Academic Skills: Follow steps to re-create Native American wearable crafts.
Teacher: Reproduce the *Mock Beaded Pocket Bag Pattern* on white and brown paper. Students should work out their colors with crayon or colored pencil on the white practice sheets before completing the final brown paper pocket bag. When painting, students must be very careful not to rest their hands on the beads of paint as they work! **Note:** Younger children can just use dots of marker.

SIOUX OR IROQUOIS MOCK BEADED POCKET BAG

Each partner completes one side of the bag to be sewn together.

Pairs Check Directions:

1. Color the white graph paper bag pattern by putting dots of color in the marked spaces.
2. Use the white pattern as your guide when making the brown bag. Carefully fill in each area with a small dot of paint. Take your time and be careful. Let it dry completely before assembling.
3. Fringe the bottom of the bag with scissors. Stay below the dotted line.
4. Sew the the two bag pieces together along the sides and and bottom with yarn in a running stitch using the dotted line as a guide
5. Punch holes at the top of the bag and string with yarn for handle. Braid the yarn for the handle, or decorate it with feathers, beads, or shells if you like.

Pocket Bag Pattern

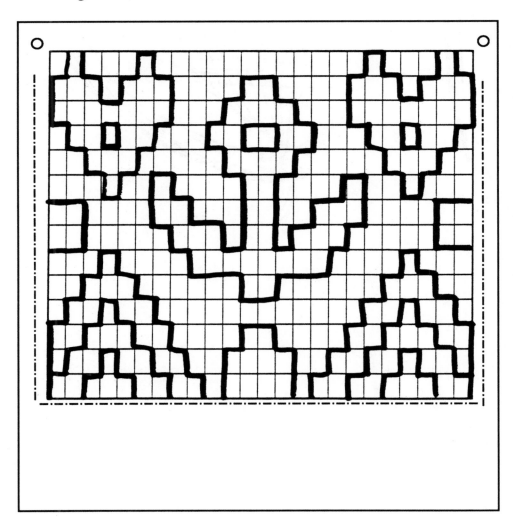

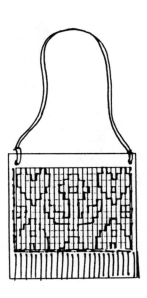

Teacher: Each group will cooperatively do a short length of weave, then sew them together with three or four other groups to make a sash. **Note:** Each group will have a different feel for weaving. They will have an appreciation of the art of getting even rows and thicknesses when they are through.

HOPI BOW-LOOM CO-OP SASHES

Teacher: Prepare a "bow" for each group. Take a 24" green bough or branch about the diameter of a finger. Curve it in a gentle bow shape and tie. When dry, it will be ready to string for weaving. Reproduce a *Sash directions* sheet for each group.

Pairs Check Directions:

Partner 1: String loom with 11 threads.

Partner 2: Weave short sticks at one end of the loom as shown.

All: Take turns weaving yarn back and forth to make the sash section.

Partner 3: When your weaving is about 12 to 14 inches long, stop and cut off of the loom. Tie off the ends, leaving extra string ends below the knots for assembly with other sashes.

Partner 4: Sew your section to another group's using a whipstitch. Add more sashes until it's the length you need.

Bow Loom

Weaving Detail

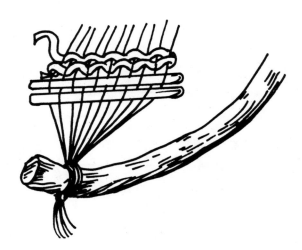

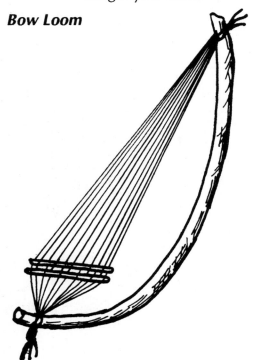

Sashes Sewn Together

IROQUOIS LEG RATTLES

Pairs Check Directions:

Partner 1: Color a rattle pattern. Glue it to a section of cardboard.

Partner 2: Cut it out. Punch open holes around edges.

Partner 1: Cut lengths of raffia or corn husks. Tie them onto the rattle at each hole. Add beads, shells, or sticks to make noise when jiggled.

Partner 2: To wear, punch black holes in the corners and string yarn for ties.

Switch roles to make the second rattle!

Leg Rattle Pattern

To Wear:

Tie below knee snugly. Bounce or shake your leg as you step or dance to make a rhythmic rattle.

IROQUOIS FALSE FACE MASK

Pairs Check Directions:

Partner 1: Paint the mask. Glue it to tagboard.

Partner 2: Cut it out. Cut eye holes carefully. Hold the mask up to your partner to make sure eye holes are spaced properly.

Partner 1: Cut 10" lengths of raffia or corn husks. Tie them to the scalp for hair.

Partner 2: Punch holes in the sides. String yarn through holes for ties.

Switch roles to do the second mask!

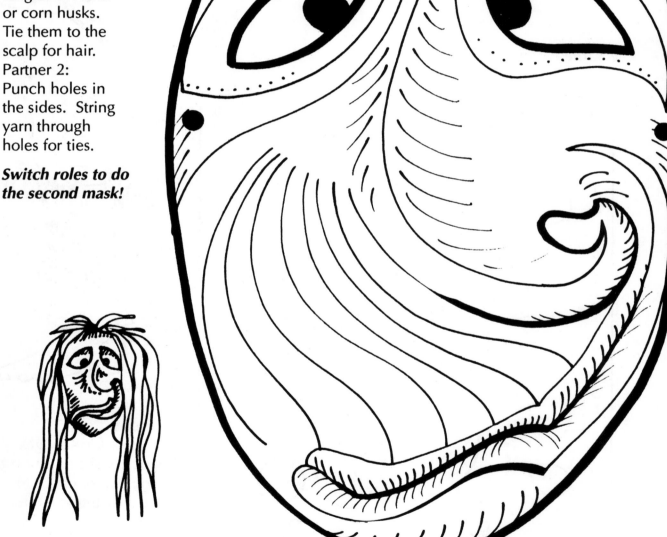

Extending Activity: FALSE FACE SOCIETY Sharing Circle
Use the mask pattern as a base to create other original designs. After all the pairs have completed their masks, gather in a sharing circle to tell the rest of the class about them. The False Face Society played an important part in Iroquois life. Find out more about the False Face Society to share in your group.

Teacher: Two batches should be enough for your class projects. Two pairs make the dough, the other pairs help shape the beads. Have students avoid touching eyes and mouth with fingers while forming beads, they are spicy and salty! On the second batch, omit the paprika for white beads. These look great with black painted details. To dry the beads for stringing, bake them gently in a 200° oven for about an hour, turning every half hour. **Note:** Fatter beads may take longer to harden.

PREPARING BEADS AND FEATHERS
HANDMADE "RED CLAY" BEADS

Pairs Check "Red Clay" Bead Recipe:
Ingredients:
1-1/4 cups flour
1-1/4 cups salt
1 cup water
2 tablespoons paprika

Directions:
Partner 1. Measure all dry ingredients and put into a big bowl.
Partner 2. Add water and mix until workable. (Add flour if it's sticky.)
Both: Form the clay into small balls and tubes (bead shapes below)
Partner 1: Use a small stick or shell to add textures to beads
Partner 2: Push a toothpick through the centers for the holes. Jiggle it around gently to make nice generous holes for stringing.

Bead Shape Suggestions:

FEATHERS FOR CRAFTING

Teacher: A variety of different feathers can be purchased in craft stores. Feathers can be used as brushes in painting, too. If real feathers cannot be obtained, use the feather patterns on page 49 to cut out paper feathers.

All Native Americans use a wide variety of feathers found in their homelands. Eagle, turkey, and macaw feathers and down decorate Hopi Kachinas, prayer sticks, and masks. Iroquois peoples create caps with topknots of eagle and egret feathers. Plains tribes are best known for their handsome war bonnets and dance bustles made from eagle, hawk, and owl feathers. Northwest Coast peoples use flicker feathers and even sea lion whiskers to add details to a chief's headdress. Feathers are more than just another craft material. They are earned through feats of courage, bravery, and adventure. They also have special significance to each tribe.

Feather Preparation Pairs Directions:
Partner 1: Soak feathers overnight in warm, soapy water.
Partner 2: Rinse in warm water. Spread them on paper towels to dry.
Both: Trim feathers to different shapes and designs as shown below.

Feather Designs:

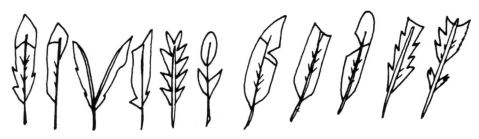

Social Skills: Positive support, vocalization, participate.
Academic Skills: Follow steps to re-create Native American wearable crafts.
Teacher: Reproduce one *Chest Plate Pattern* to be completed by each group.

PLAINS CHEST PLATE

Study Group Directions:

Partner 1: Gather materials to make one chest plate: 4 fat soda straws (cut in half), 6 cords, beads, shells, and feathers.

Partner 2: Use the strip pattern to trace and cut out 3 strips. Punch (open) holes as shown.

Partners 3, 4, 1, 2: String one row of the chest plate by tying and stringing the materials as shown onto the cords and through the strips. Put one piece of straw in each section between a bead, shell, or feather on each end.

Partner 3: Tie one cord to top of outside chest plate strip as shown on the finished chest plate.

Partner 4: Tie the other cord to top of the other chest plate strip.

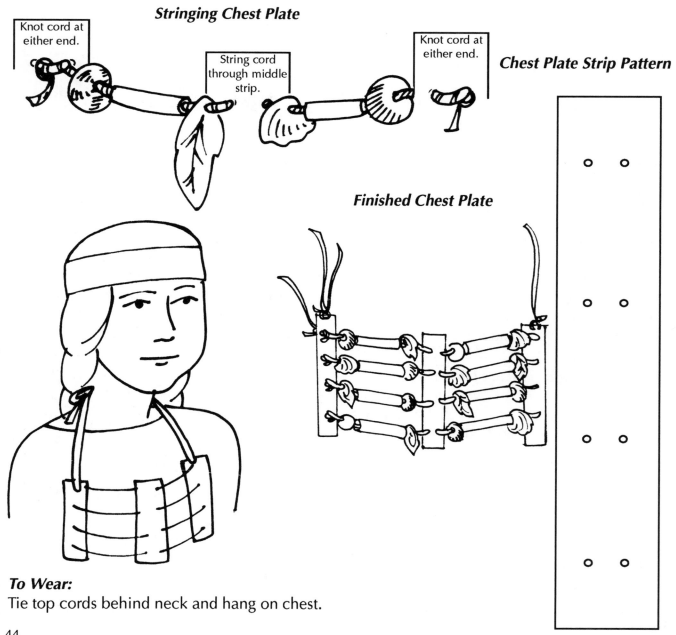

Stringing Chest Plate

Knot cord at either end.

String cord through middle strip.

Knot cord at either end.

Chest Plate Strip Pattern

Finished Chest Plate

To Wear:
Tie top cords behind neck and hang on chest.

Teacher: Reproduce one *Pendant and Belt Buckle Pattern* for each pair. They will take turns completing one, then switch roles for the second craft.

SOUTHWEST "SILVER" PENDANT AND BELT BUCKLE

Pairs Check Directions:

Partner 1: Cut one of the shapes out of cardboard or tagboard.

Partner 2: Cover the shape with 2–3 layers of aluminum foil.

Partner 1: Use a stick, pencil, or shell to create patterns in the foil.
Gently press and poke the tool into your shape. The decorated designs shown will get you started. Be careful not to tear the foil. (If that happens, just cover with another layer of foil and start again.) Experiment making different patterns with your tools.

Partner 2: Cut a length of cord, and string the pendant onto it to wear. (**Note:** The belt buckle is not strong enough to be worn alone. Tape it on top of your belt.)

Switch roles to make the second project!

Pendant Base

Pendant Design Pattern

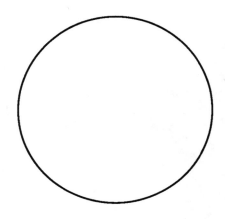

Buckle Base

Buckle Design pattern

Other Design Suggestions

zigzag rows   slanted lines   leaves   dotted lines

Social Skills: Positive support, elaborate, participate.
Academic Skills: Follow steps to re-create Native American wearable crafts.
Teacher: Reproduce one *Bear Mask Pattern* for each group. Before mask is mounted, have roundtable groups work on the mask, putting their initials in pencil in a section as it passes. Keep going until all the spaces are filled. Use the initials as a guide when passing the mask to glue on the yarn. As with the *False Face Mask,* do not use the completed *Bear Mask* as a toy. Treat it with honor and pride as a tribal relic.

NORTHWEST BEAR MASK

Round Table Directions:

1. Glue mask pattern to tagboard. Cut out eye holes.
2. Take turns filling in one initialed section at a time. Glue yarn down in even, circular patterns.
3. Keep passing the mask and gluing the yarn sections until it is complete.

Bear Mask Pattern

Yarn Detail

Social Skills: Positive support, elaborate, participate
Academic Skills: Follow steps to re-create Native American wearable crafts.
Teacher: Reproduce one set of *Feather Headdress Band Pattern* pages for each group and one sheet of *Headdress Feathers* for each member. Use a different color of paper for each sheet of feathers.

SIOUX WARRIOR HEADDRESS

Sioux Warrior's Headdress Band 1
Cut out and glue as shown to band 2.

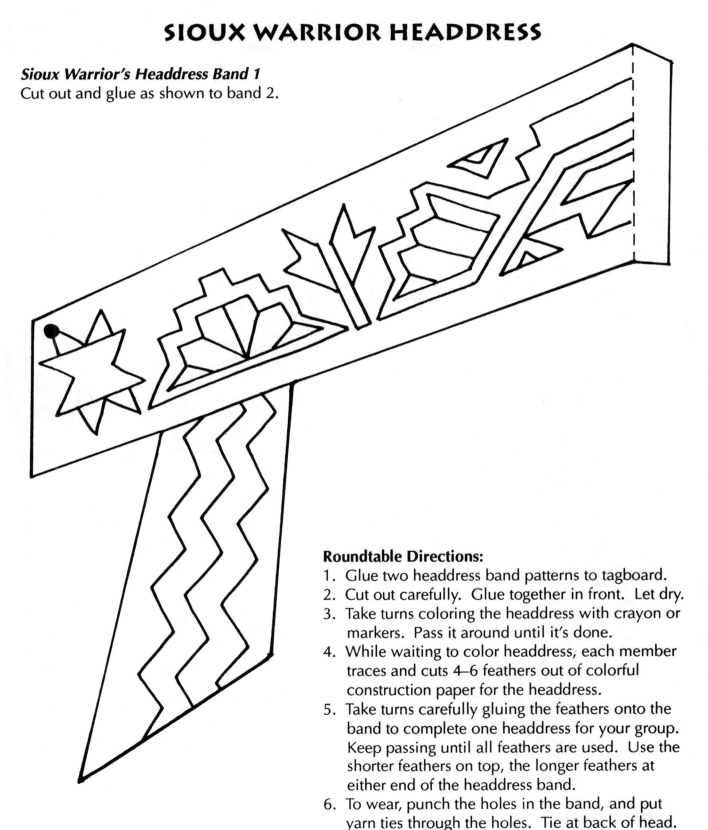

Roundtable Directions:
1. Glue two headdress band patterns to tagboard.
2. Cut out carefully. Glue together in front. Let dry.
3. Take turns coloring the headdress with crayon or markers. Pass it around until it's done.
4. While waiting to color headdress, each member traces and cuts 4–6 feathers out of colorful construction paper for the headdress.
5. Take turns carefully gluing the feathers onto the band to complete one headdress for your group. Keep passing until all feathers are used. Use the shorter feathers on top, the longer feathers at either end of the headdress band.
6. To wear, punch the holes in the band, and put yarn ties through the holes. Tie at back of head.

Sioux Warrior's Headdress Band 2
Cut out and glue as shown to band 1.

Completed Sioux Warrior's Headdress
Glue feathers in place as shown;
smaller ones in the center,
larger ones at outer edges.

To Wear Headdress:
Put yarn ties through holes as shown and tie at back of head.

Teacher: Use cleaned, prepared feathers in place of paper feathers if you have them from the decorative crafts activity on page 43. Or trim the paper feathers in some of the ways suggested on that page. Reproduce *Headdress Feathers* in 4 colors for each group.

Headdress Feathers

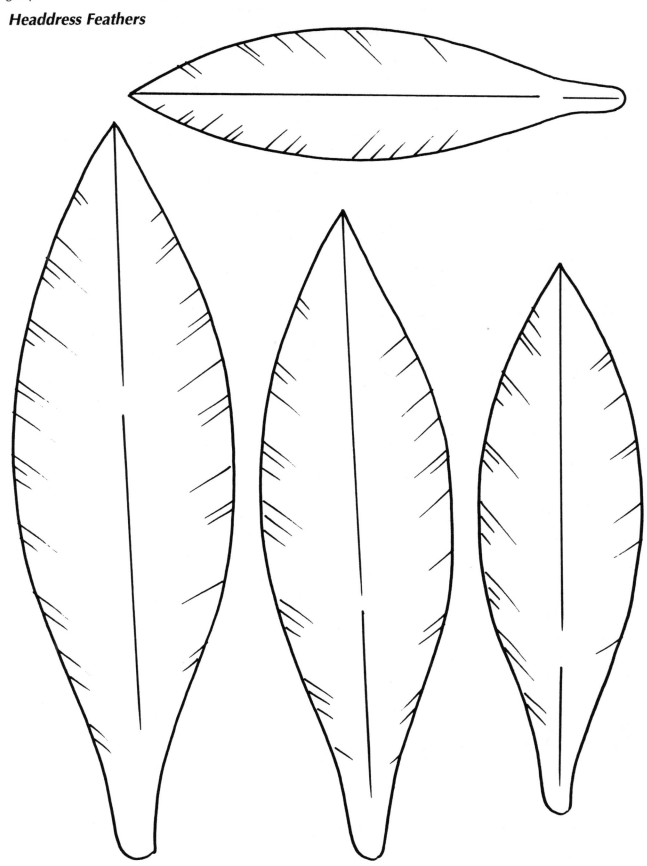

CHAPTER 3: SURVIVING IN THE ENVIRONMENT

Native Americans live all over the continent. Where they live determines what they eat and what tools and utensils they make to help in their day-to-day lives. Remember that all Native Americans have to make everything they need from what they find in their habitats or trade things they have with other tribes.

The tools created are similar from one area to another. They may be made of varying materials, but they have the same uses. All the tribes we are studying make baskets from grasses, reeds or wood strips. All use animal skins and fur. All make pottery, except the Nootkas in the Northwest.

1. DANCING SQUIRREL (OJIBWA)

We hunt our food in the vast birch forests in the Northeast. We hunt along rivers and streams where animals go to drink. We use birchbark canoes to travel the rivers to find wild game, to fish, and to gather plants to eat. Men and boys hunt for meat. Women and girls gather plants, seeds, wild rice, and nuts. All our tools are made of stone, bone, or wood.

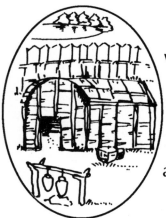

2. GOLDEN FAWN (IROQUOIS)

We live in a village in the forests of the Northeast. Corn, beans, squash, and tobacco are grown in our fields. The men clear the fields of trees, but women plant and tend the crops. Women also gather nuts and fruits from the forests. Men hunt for meat and trap fish. Our tools are made of stone, bone, and wood.

3. WHITE CLAY (CHEROKEE)

We live in the mountain forests in the Southeast. Corn, beans, squash, gourds, and tobacco grow in our fields. Men hunt in the deep forests and trap fish in the rivers. We live along the river banks and make dugout canoes to travel the rivers. Our tools are made of stone, bone, wood, and large seashells.

4. TALL GRASS WAVING (SIOUX)

Our tribe roams the vast plains in the center of the continent. We do not plant any crops because we are never in one place long enough to grow them. Our whole existence depends on the buffalo. Each person in our camp eats about three pounds of buffalo meat each day. Men hunt the buffalo and women make everything we need from them. Our tools are made of stone, bone, and wood.

Before horses were brought in by the Spanish (1598), our only helping animal was the dog. Dogs could not pull much weight on a travois, a platform on poles used for dragging things. Travel was hard and we had to walk everywhere. My grandfather tells about the first time a Sioux saw a horse. He called it Big Dog because we had no word for the animal. The Sioux quickly mastered horseback riding. Now horses pull our travois, help us in the hunt, and help us travel quickly. Our tipis can be larger because horses can pull longer poles than dogs.

5. RAIN IN HER HAIR (HOPI)

The Hopi hunt birds, rabbits, and deer for feathers and meat. We live in the desert, where there is little large game. We plant crops of corn, beans, squash, and cotton. The men tend the crops and weave the cloth. Women build most of the houses and make the food. Our tools are made of stone, bone, and wood.

6. RAVEN'S BEAK (NOOTKA)

We live in the rainy Northwest. Food is so plentiful here that we do not need to plant crops. We gather nuts, fruits, and other plants in the forests. Cedar trees provide us with almost everything we need. Our people are good fishermen. We build huge canoes so we can harpoon whales. Men trap salmon in the rushing streams. We catch enough fish in the summer so that we do not have to work in the winter. Our tools are made of wood, bone, and stone.

Teacher: Some of the co-op cards in this chapter are coded with the following numbers to indicate which tribes use the item illustrated. Help children choose the cards they need for each activity.
1. Dancing Squirrel—Ojibwa 2. Golden Fawn—Iroquois 3. White Clay—Cherokee
4. Tall Grass Waving—Sioux 5. Rain in Her Hair—Hopi 6. Raven's Beak—Nootka

Social Skill: Seek accuracy, participate, ask for help when needed, extend another's answers
Academic Skill: Formulate a game based on habitat and hunting habits of various tribes.
Teacher: Each group chooses a tribe to study. Children will use the co-op cards that are appropriate for the area of the country where tribes reside. The cards are numbered to help children gather those needed. Reproduce one set of co-op cards for each group.

TO THE HUNT!

Choose a tribe to study. Each group member takes one role card and follows the directions on it. Work together to create a board game or picture about hunting game, birds, and fish. Play the game together.

ROLE CARD 1:

Describe the area where your tribe hunts for food. Gather the co-op cards that show the trees and plants in the area.

ROLE CARD 2:

List the animals that are hunted for food in your area. Gather the co-op cards that show the animals.

ROLE CARD 3:

Create a trail game using the information. Get help from group members 1, 2, and 4.

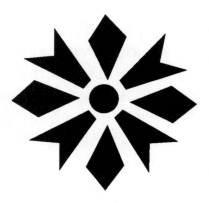

ROLE CARD 4:

Working with group members, write the directions for your game.

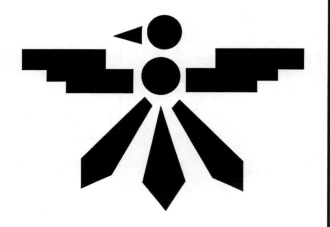

 Extending Activity: Share your game with another group. Both groups play each game.

52

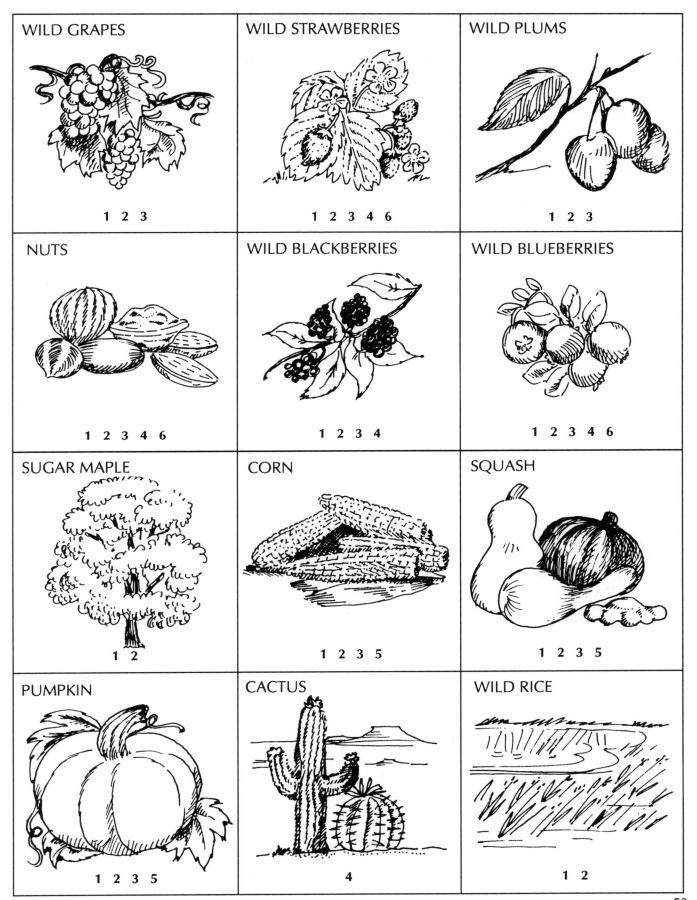

WILD GRAPES

1 2 3

WILD STRAWBERRIES

1 2 3 4 6

WILD PLUMS

1 2 3

NUTS

1 2 3 4 6

WILD BLACKBERRIES

1 2 3 4

WILD BLUEBERRIES

1 2 3 4 6

SUGAR MAPLE

1 2

CORN

1 2 3 5

SQUASH

1 2 3 5

PUMPKIN

1 2 3 5

CACTUS

4

WILD RICE

1 2

Hunting Co-op Cards

BEAR
1 2 3 6

BEAVER
1 2 3

BUFFALO
3

DEER
1 2 3 4 5 6

DUCK
1 2 3

EEL
1 2

ELK
1 2

GOOSE
1 2 3

MOOSE
1 2

OPOSSUM
1 2 3

OTTER
6

QUAIL
1 2 3

RABBIT
1 2 3 4 5 6

SALMON
6

SEAL
6

SQUIRREL
1 2 3 5 6

STURGEON
1 2

TURKEY
1 2 3

WHALE
6

TROUT
1 2 3

RACCOON
1 2 3

FOX
1 2 3

EAGLE
1 2 3 4 5 6

PHEASANT
1 2 3

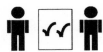

Recipes are used with permission from *Native American Recipes for the Classroom* by Dr. Karen Harvey of Littleton, Ohio.

COOKING THE CORN

The Hopi have more that fifty ways to prepare corn. All the tribes we're studying except the Nootka use corn. In years past corn was cooked over an open fire, on a stone griddle or in a pit oven in the ground. Work together to prepare one of the following recipes to share with other groups. Find other Native American recipes to share and prepare.

SUCCOTASH

4–6 strips bacon
1 chopped onion
1/4 cup chopped green pepper
2 cups cooked corn
2 cups cooked lima beans

Partner 1: Fry the bacon. Drain the fat.
Partner 2: Add the onion and green peppers.
Partner 1: When the onion is golden brown, add the corn and lima beans.
Partner 2: Cover and simmer about 10 minutes. Add salt and pepper to taste.

BEAN BREAD

2 cups cornmeal
1 teaspoon salt
1 teaspoon baking powder
2 eggs
1 1/2 cups milk
2 cups cooked brown beans, drained

Partner 1: Mix together dry ingredients.
Partner 2: Add eggs and milk.
Partner 1: Stir in drained beans.
Partner 2: Pour into a greased pan or iron skillet.

Bake at 450° for 20–25 minutes or until brown.

Social Skills: Integrate ideas into one, work toward a goal, ask for help when needed.
Academic Skills: Plan and preserve food following a recipe.
Teacher: This assignment should be done in pairs at home. Children bring the food to school to share.

PRESERVING FOOD

Native Americans are very resourceful in preserving food. Many foods are dried by hanging out in the open air. The Meat Jerky below is hung out in the full sun for several days to dry. The recipe below is a modern method that will give you quicker results. Work together to follow a recipe. Bring the results to school to share.

LEATHER BRITCHES

1 pound green beans, washed
1/4 pound bacon, chopped
2 teaspoons salt
1/8 teaspoon ground pepper

Snap the ends off the beans and string on heavy thread. Hang in a sunny place to dry for two months. When you are ready to cook the beans, soak them for one hour in 2 quarts of water. Add the bacon, salt, and pepper and bring to a boil. Reduce heat and simmer very slowly, stirring occasionally, for three hours. Add water if necessary. Serve hot with broth. Corn bread is good to sop up the liquid.

MEAT JERKY

3 pounds of any meat
Liquid Smoke, if desired

Trim fat from meat and cut into strips about 1/8" thick. Hang the meat on a wire rack in a baking pan. Put the meat into preheated oven at 160° to 175° and leave until it is crisp and stiff. If there is any doubt that the jerky is done, turn off the heat and leave the meat in the oven overnight. Brushing oven-dried meat with Liquid Smoke gives it an outdoor touch.

PEMMICAN

Pemmican is such a concentrated food that it is a staple among the Plains peoples, particularly for use on long journeys. Jerky is pounded until it is powder dry. Melted fat and dried berries or maple syrup are then pounded into it to make a sweet paste. Roll into balls in palm of hand. As the fat cools it becomes solid.

Social Skills: Use names, be positive, jog memory.
Academic Skills: Learn about the uses of typical tools.
Teacher: Reproduce cards and *Co-op Cards* from pages 58–60 for each group.

NATIVE AMERICAN TOOLS

Pick a tribe to study. Think about the environment where you live. What do you think you would make your tools from? How would you use your tools? Hard metals such as iron or steel are not available. Tools are made of stone, bone, antler, wood, or shells. Rope or twine for holding tools together is made of bark fibers, leather strips, or animal sinew. Choose four different tools from the co-op cards that have your number on them. Take turns filling in a card for each tool.

FILL-IN TOOL CARD 1

Tool Name: _____

What it is made of: _____

_____

_____

What it is used for: _____

_____

FILL-IN TOOL CARD 2

Tool Name: _____

What it is made of: _____

_____

_____

What it is used for: _____

_____

FILL-IN TOOL CARD 3

Tool Name: _____

What it is made of: _____

_____

_____

What it is used for: _____

_____

FILL-IN TOOL CARD 4

Tool Name: _____

What it is made of: _____

_____

_____

What it is used for: _____

_____

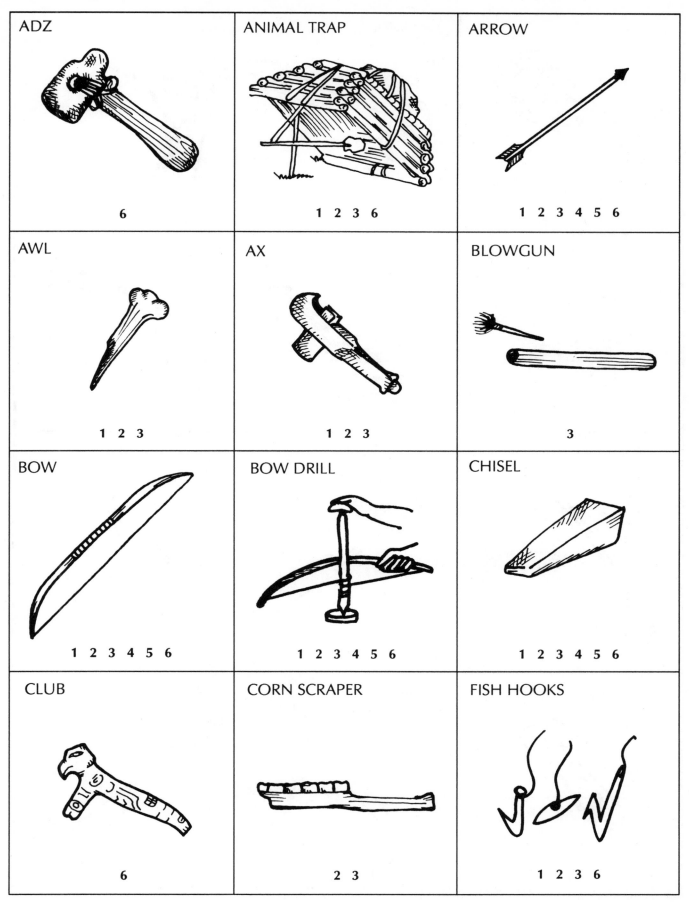

ADZ	ANIMAL TRAP	ARROW
6	1 2 3 6	1 2 3 4 5 6

AWL	AX	BLOWGUN
1 2 3	1 2 3	3

BOW	BOW DRILL	CHISEL
1 2 3 4 5 6	1 2 3 4 5 6	1 2 3 4 5 6

CLUB	CORN SCRAPER	FISH HOOKS
6	2 3	1 2 3 6

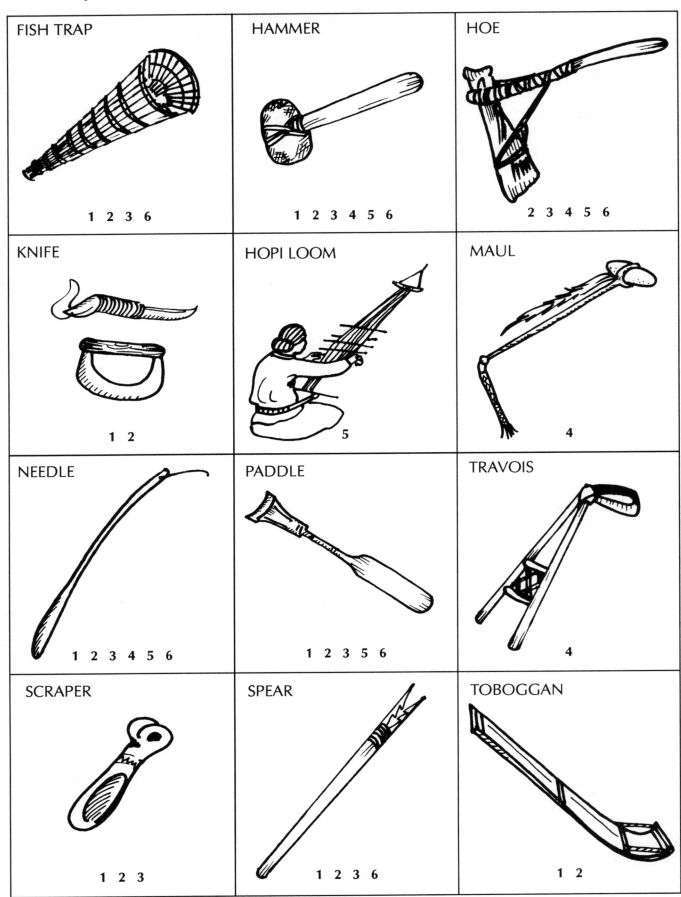

FISH TRAP	HAMMER	HOE
1 2 3 6	1 2 3 4 5 6	2 3 4 5 6
KNIFE	HOPI LOOM	MAUL
1 2	5	4
NEEDLE	PADDLE	TRAVOIS
1 2 3 4 5 6	1 2 3 5 6	4
SCRAPER	SPEAR	TOBOGGAN
1 2 3	1 2 3 6	1 2

Social Skills: Participate, no put-downs, seek accuracy.
Academic Skills: Decorate a basket using an appropriate design.
Teacher: Show baskets in the classroom. Reproduce the sheets for each pair.

BUSHELS OF BASKETS

Every group except the buffalo hunters make baskets. They are made of grass, wood splints, wicker, roots, bark fiber, or corn husks. They are used for storage, cooking, carrying water, and gathering food. Choose a basket shape for a specific tribe and decorate it with a proper design.

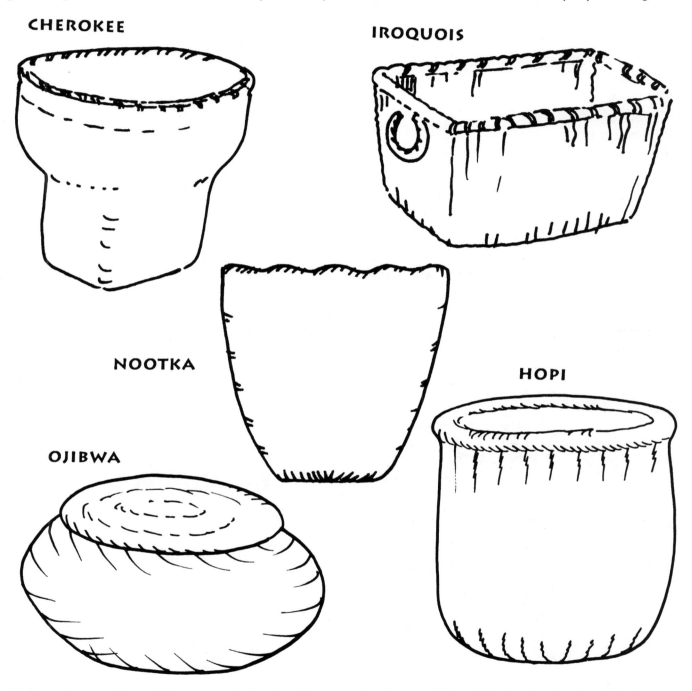

CHEROKEE

IROQUOIS

NOOTKA

HOPI

OJIBWA

Extending Activity: Bring in baskets from home. Look at them carefully and decide what they are made of. Discuss how they are made by weaving in different ways.

Extending Activity: Ask a basket weaver to come into the classroom and demonstrate how baskets are made.

Social Skills: Work toward a goal, integrate a number of ideas, no put-downs.
Academic Skills: Follow steps to create several pottery designs.
Teacher: Provide self-drying clay and various textures for designs.

DESIGNING POTTERY

Every group except the Nootkas makes pottery. Some of it is left plain for everyday use. Other pieces are decorated with special designs. They can be impressed with other materials, scratched on with a sharp tool, or stamped. You will be designing on clay for this project.

Materials:
Balls of damp clay
Wax paper
dry corncob
dry ear of corn
onion bag netting
heavy twine or rope
pencil or cuticle stick

Directions:
1. Each person in the pair chooses one material for making a design on the clay.
2. Place clay balls on a piece of wax paper. Press ball of clay into a rectangular shape about 1/4" thick.
3. Decorate clay by pressing the corn, netting, or twine into it. Do not leave materials embedded in clay. Or use a pencil to scratch in a design like the examples shown.   The design is finished when both agree it is done.
4. Allow clay to dry on wax paper.   Remove wax paper.

Extending Activity: Find examples of painted pottery. Choose a design you both like. Draw a piece of pottery and paint it with the design.

Social Skills: Stay in group, plan quietly, summarize goals.
Academic Skills: Follow the steps to create Native American campsites.
Teacher: Reproduce *Homes and Furnishings* for each group. Put completed scenes with the homes projects from Chapter 1.

FURNISHING A HOME

Choose a scene for each member of the group. Cut it out and glue it to a larger sheet of plain paper. Color and cut out furnishings and give some to each member. Pass the scenes around the group. Glue furnishing on and around the appropriate scenes.

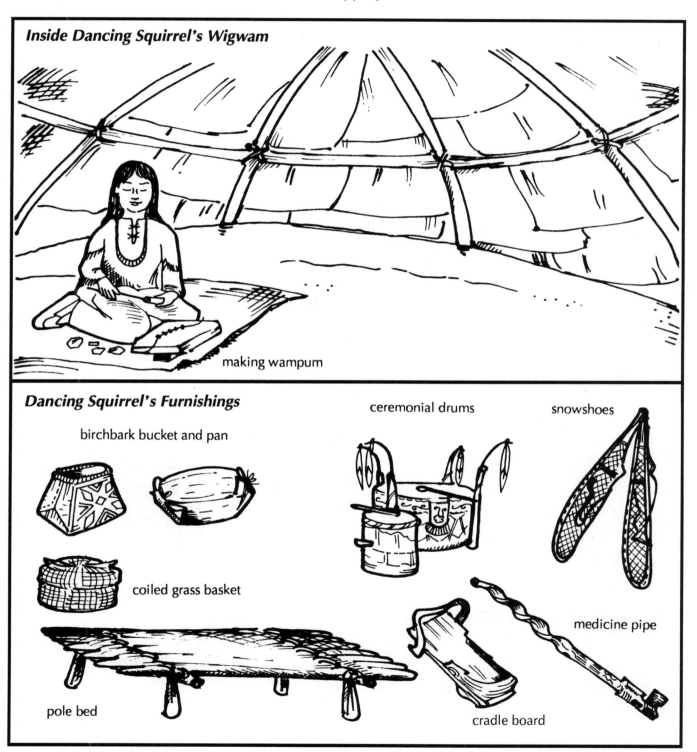

Inside Dancing Squirrel's Wigwam

making wampum

Dancing Squirrel's Furnishings

birchbark bucket and pan

ceremonial drums

snowshoes

coiled grass basket

pole bed

cradle board

medicine pipe

Inside Golden Fawn's Long House

cooking stew

Golden Fawn's Furnishings

water drum

cradle board

clay pot with scratched design

braided corn husk bottle

ashwood basket with squash

tumpline to carry loads

deerskin

carved wooden bowl and spoon
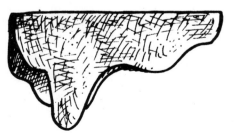

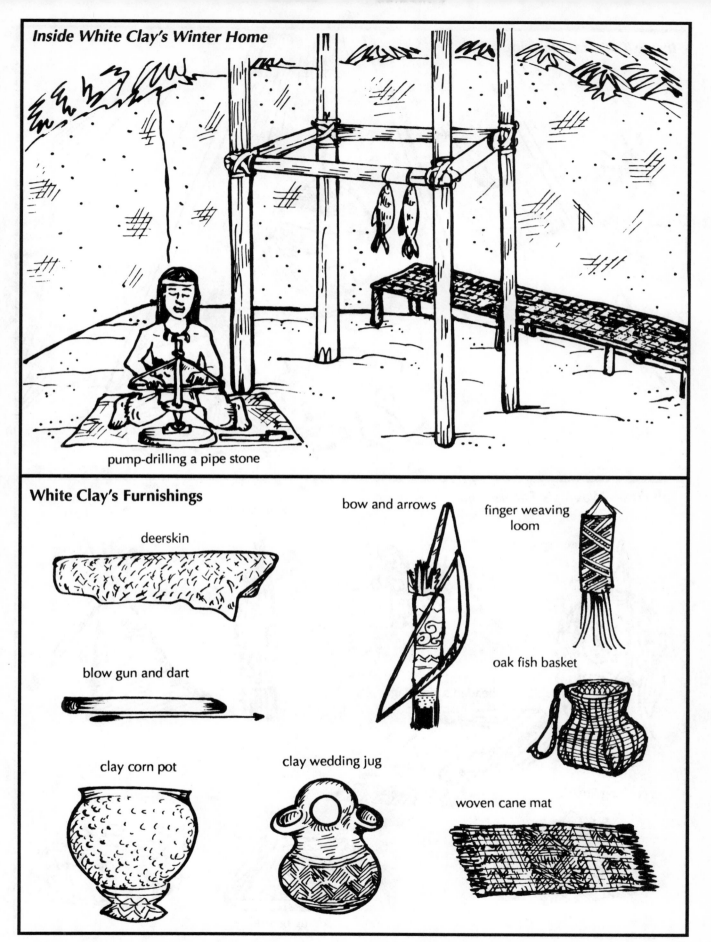

Inside White Clay's Winter Home

pump-drilling a pipe stone

White Clay's Furnishings

deerskin

bow and arrows

finger weaving loom

blow gun and dart

oak fish basket

clay corn pot

clay wedding jug

woven cane mat

Inside Tall Grass Waving's Tipi

making moccasins

Tall Grass Waving's Furnishings

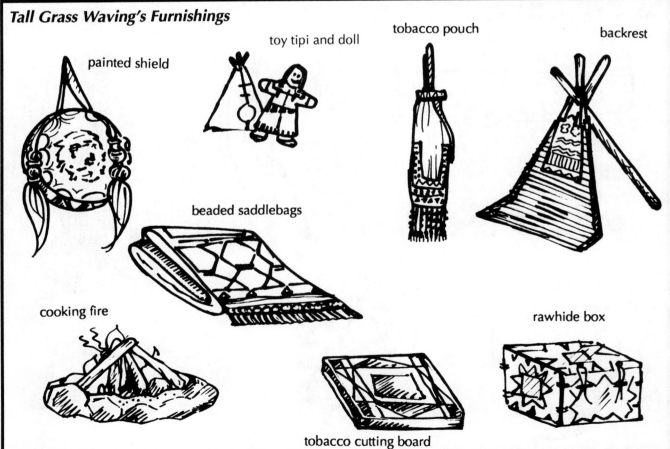

painted shield

toy tipi and doll

tobacco pouch

backrest

beaded saddlebags

cooking fire

tobacco cutting board

rawhide box

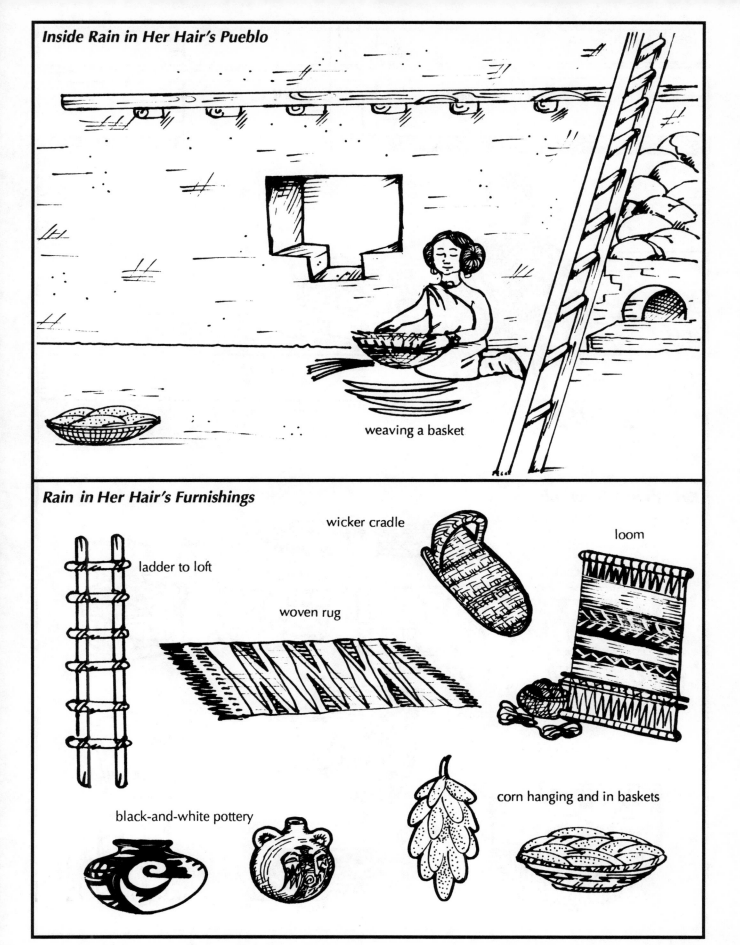

Inside Rain in Her Hair's Pueblo

weaving a basket

Rain in Her Hair's Furnishings

ladder to loft

wicker cradle

loom

woven rug

black-and-white pottery

corn hanging and in baskets

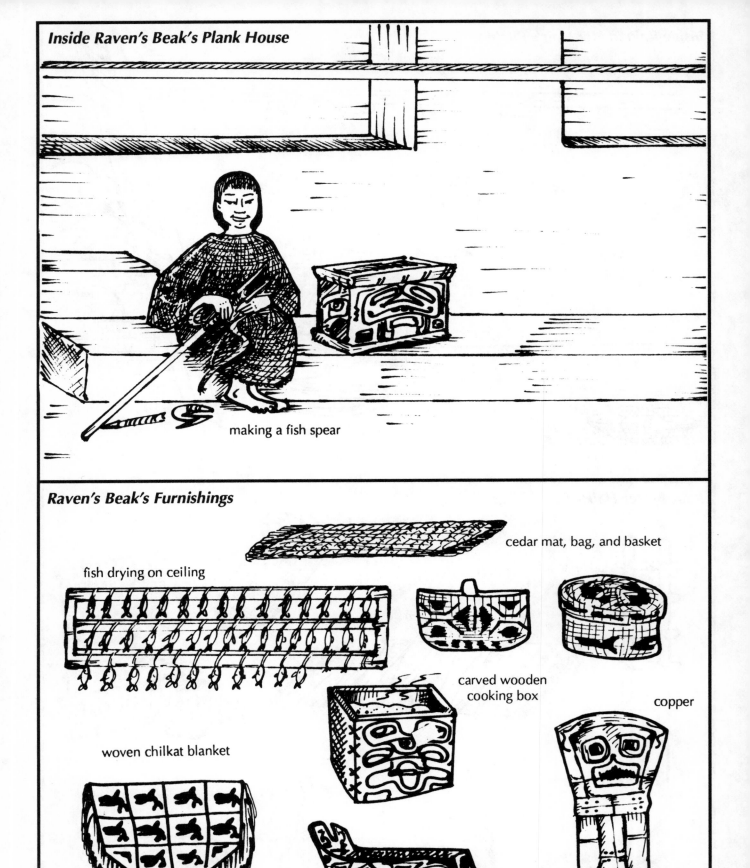

Inside Raven's Beak's Plank House

making a fish spear

Raven's Beak's Furnishings

cedar mat, bag, and basket

fish drying on ceiling

carved wooden cooking box

copper

woven chilkat blanket

carved wooden cradle

Social Skills: Work toward a goal, elaborate, stay in group.
Academic Skills: Follow steps to create a story in sequence.
Teacher: Adding machine tape will work well for this project.

BUFFALO HUNT STORY STRIPS

Hunting for buffalo is a group effort. No one is allowed to hunt alone. The welfare of the whole village depends on a successful hunt. Cut out the *Story Strips*. Paste them on a strip of paper. Illustrate the *Story Strips* with pictographs. Decide on the proper order for the story. Glue the strips end to end to tell the whole story of your hunt. Share your story with another group.

Scouts ride out on the plains looking for a buffalo herd.

The chief and council smoke a pipe and pray for the safety of the hunters.

A herd is spotted and the scouts ride back to tell the chief.

A ceremony with dancing and singing celebrates the end of a successful hunt.

Hunters decorate their bodies with paint to show respect for the buffalo.

The chief and the council tell the hunters to begin the hunt.

The hunters ride into the buffalo herd with their lances and bows and arrows.

Women prepare a feast with the fresh buffalo meat.

Social Skills: Use quiet voices, listen actively.
Academic Skills: Discuss, ask questions, and write the many uses of the buffalo for the Sioux.
Teacher: Reproduce one chart for each group.

BUFFALO, THE GREAT PROVIDER FOR THE SIOUX

The buffalo is not only a source of meat for the Sioux. It provides them with everything they need to survive in the Great Plains. Every part has some use. The word list tells some uses for buffalo. Discuss them in your group. Pass the sheet around and take turns writing words under each heading. Cross out words as they are used. The numbers tell how many words to write.

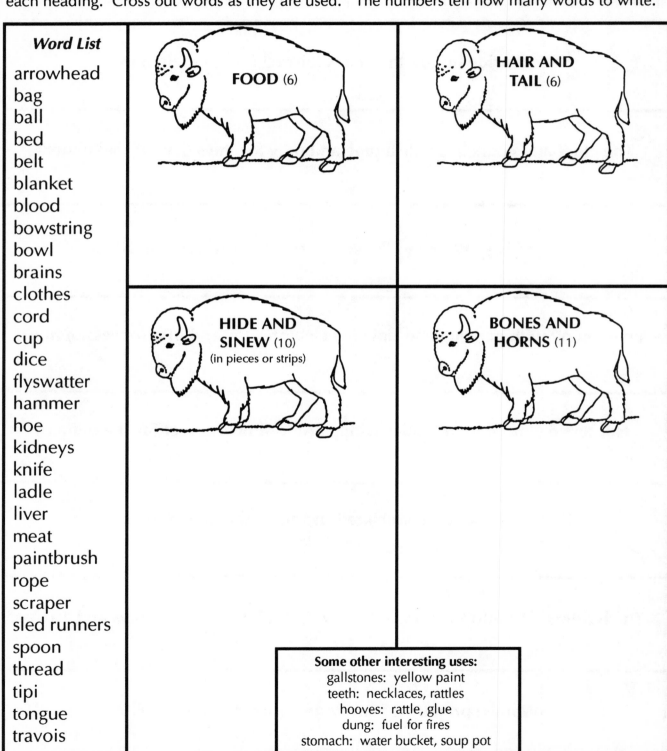

Word List

arrowhead
bag
ball
bed
belt
blanket
blood
bowstring
bowl
brains
clothes
cord
cup
dice
flyswatter
hammer
hoe
kidneys
knife
ladle
liver
meat
paintbrush
rope
scraper
sled runners
spoon
thread
tipi
tongue
travois

FOOD (6)

HAIR AND TAIL (6)

HIDE AND SINEW (10)
(in pieces or strips)

BONES AND HORNS (11)

Some other interesting uses:
gallstones: yellow paint
teeth: necklaces, rattles
hooves: rattle, glue
dung: fuel for fires
stomach: water bucket, soup pot

Social Skills: Extend another's answers, vocalize, no put-downs.
Academic Skills: Create a group list of the uses of cedar by the Nootkas.
Teacher: Reproduce one sheet for each group.

CEDAR, THE GREAT PROVIDER FOR THE NOOTKA

The cedar tree for the Nootkas is similar to the buffalo for the Sioux. It provides them their houses and almost all their furnishings. List the items at the bottom of the page under what they are made from in the *Cedar Chart* below.

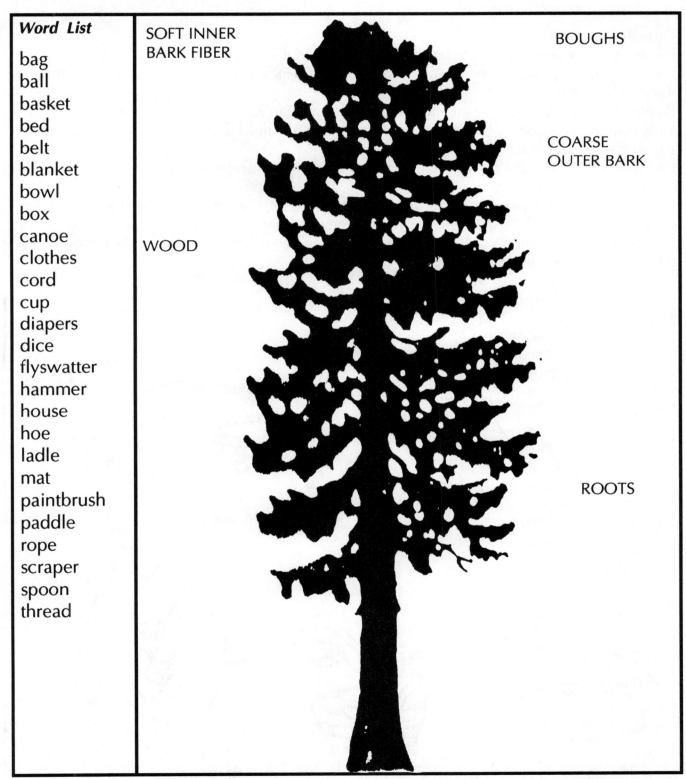

Word List

bag
ball
basket
bed
belt
blanket
bowl
box
canoe
clothes
cord
cup
diapers
dice
flyswatter
hammer
house
hoe
ladle
mat
paintbrush
paddle
rope
scraper
spoon
thread

SOFT INNER BARK FIBER

BOUGHS

COARSE OUTER BARK

WOOD

ROOTS

Social Skills: Form groups quietly, participate, ask for help.
Academic Skills: Follow directions to make a clay dish.
Teacher: Provide pairs with self-drying clay and wax paper.

NATIVE AMERICAN CRAFTS

The Hopi make coiled pottery. Work together to make a small clay dish. Put clay on a sheet of wax paper. Wet your hands with water while working with the clay.

Directions:
Partner 1: Pat a piece of damp clay into a 3" circle about 1/4" thick for the pot base.
Partner 2: Roll pieces of clay into coils between your hands as shown. They should be about as thick as your finger.
Partner 1: Take a coil of clay and lay it around the clay circle.
Partner 2: Add another coil on top of the first one. Pinch the clay between your fingers to make the coils stick together.
Both: Take turns making coils of clay and adding to top of the others. Overlap coils and pinch them together as you go.
Partner 1: When the pot is about 2" tall, gently squeeze the clay between your fingers to make the pot the same thickness all around. Turning the pot as you work makes shaping easier.
Partner 2: Smooth out any cracks or uneven areas with your fingers on the inside and outside of the pot. Turn the pot as you work.

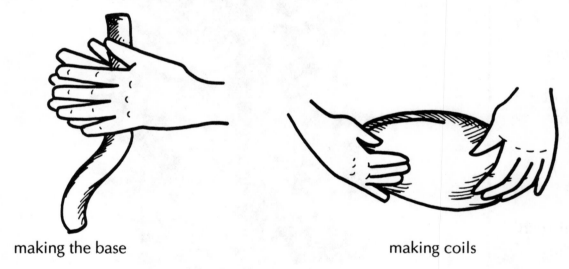

making the base   making coils

adding coils   smoothing the pot

Social Skills: Work quietly, integrate ideas, work toward a goal.
Academic Skill: Design and construct a paper envelope.
Teacher: Reproduce on tagboard.

MAKING A PARFLECHE

A parfleche is a large envelope of rawhide used by the Sioux to pack dried food and other things. Rawhide is untanned buffalo skin. When it is wet it can be bent and molded. For the Sioux it takes the place of pottery, wood, and bark. Work together to make a paper parfleche. You may want to store your co-op cards inside.

Materials:
parfleche pattern
scissors
markers
yarn or cord

Parfleche Pattern

Directions:
1. Cut out the parfleche pattern.
2. Turn the pattern over to the blank side. Color in a pretty design with markers.
3. Punch holes on the dots. String with yarn as shown.
4. Fold the parfleche on the dotted lines. Your design should be on the outside.

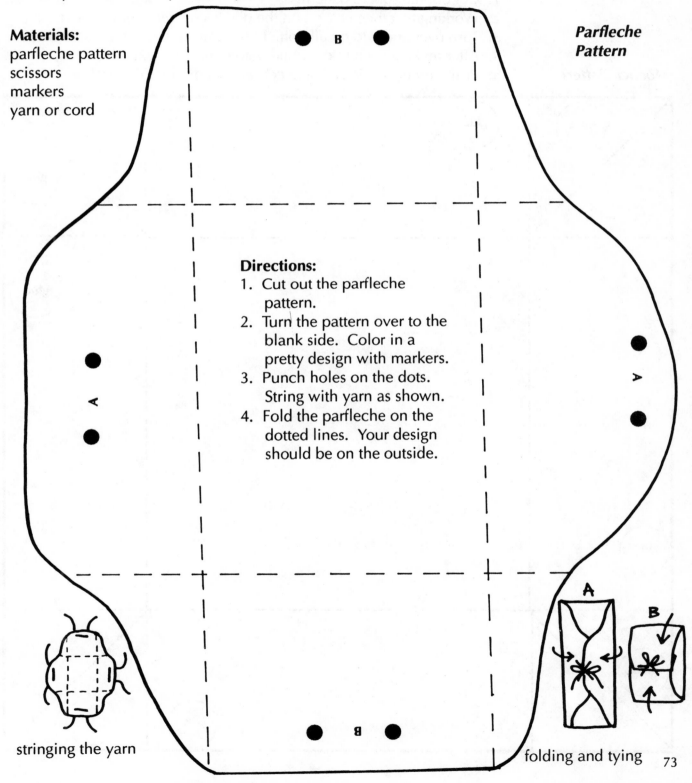

stringing the yarn

folding and tying

73

Social Skills: Work toward a goal, ask for help when needed.
Academic Skill: Design and make a mocuck box.
Teacher: Reproduce pattern on tagboard.

FOLDING MOCUCK

The Ojibwa make storage boxes called mocucks from woven mats.

Directions:
1. Cut out the square pattern.
2. Working together, color it on the blank side with geometric designs.
3. Turn over and fold on all dotted lines toward the center of the box.
4. After making each fold, unfold before making next fold.
5. Push corners to sides. Glue corners to box sides on circles.

Mocuck Pattern

glue

glue

glue

glue

glue

glue

glue

glue

glue

CHAPTER 4:
HOW DID THE PEOPLES COMMUNICATE?

TALL GRASS WAVING (SIOUX)

There is a quiet breeze blowing across the grasses of the Great Plains tonight. Many tribes of the Sioux nation have gathered this summer for a powwow. Our tipis are set in circles around the huge council lodge tipi. They are new and almost white. Our fires inside make the tipis glow across the prairie. The council lodge seems deserted except for the firelight that glows in the doorway, but there are many men inside. The chiefs and warriors are silent as the pipe is passed from man to man. It is polite to remain silent at the beginning of a visit. It would be rude to speak until after the pipe is passed.

After the pipe is passed, chiefs begin to talk among themselves, but people of different tribes speak different languages and do not understand one another. In the council lodge, one man stands as if to speak, but he does not. He starts to gesture with his hands in sign language. All the Native Americans understand sign language. There are signs for every word. I am learning sign language from my grandfather. Sometimes he does not allow me to speak at all, so that I will have to make myself understood using only hand signs. He is proud of me for learning well. When I am older and out wandering across the plains, I will be able to talk to anyone I meet.

RAVEN'S BEAK (NOOTKA)

Native Americans have no written language, so storytelling is very important. Chiefs and grandfathers tell stories of the history, religion, and battles of our ancestors in the tribe. We learn about ourselves and what is expected of us through stories. Stories are passed down to each generation. When I am a man I will tell stories to my children. Other Northwest peoples use totem poles to tell stories about their chief's brave deeds or those of his ancestors.

HOW NATIVE AMERICANS COMMUNICATE WITH ONE ANOTHER

•Communicating by the Spoken Word:

The language of Native Americans is based on pictures and symbols. Indians think in terms of pictures. Native American languages are perfectly adapted to their needs. In many ways they are able to convey more information with fewer words. In the Cherokee language a single word may incorporate all the elements of a sentence. For instance, GADAWO'A means "I am washing myself," while GAGUN'SGWO'A means "I am washing my face." The vocabulary of a tribe directly reflects life and the things around them. A Woodland person has a lot more words for wood and trees. Southwest and Plains peoples have a richer ceremonial vocabulary.

Greetings:

HAU KOLA
(good friend)

SE GO LI
(good morning)

SKA NOH
(more power to you)

• Communicating by Storytelling:

Storytelling entertains, instructs, and empowers people to live in a good relationship with their world and neighbors. Storytellers are well-respected, older relatives—perhaps a grandparent, aunt, or uncle. Iroquois tribes have professional storytellers called HAGEOTA, "one who tells stories." Storytellers often use a pouch filled with props such as claws, feathers, a corn husk doll, an arrowhead, or other objects to help them remember and tell a particular legend.

• Communicating by the Use of Signs and Symbols:

Many of the tribes of North America speak different languages. Native Americans would have a very hard time talking to any stranger they meet if they did not have sign language. Tribal sign language is sort of like signing for the deaf. Sign language is the world's most easily learned language. It has mostly nouns and verbs. Most of the signs are made with the right hand. Because it is so basic and flexible, it is possible for many different tribes with different languages to communicate with one another.

• Communicating by the Use of Wampum:

Wampum is not only a form of money, but it's also a means of communication used by the Iroquois and Ojibwa tribes. It is made from white and purple clam and quahog shells. Strings of wampum are used to exchange goods and are sometimes even used as identification. Belts of wampum are used to record important treaties and events.

•Communicating Through Arts:

Some Northwest peoples communicate through their totem symbols. It is a spectacular way to show off and explain their own history to other tribes. Totems are not idols of worship. They tell stories about a particular tribe's history or stories that a clan owns. Another powerful way Native Americans communicate is through songs and dances. Your librarian will be able to help you find books and records about Native American ceremonies, music, and dances.

Social Skills: Speak clearly, listen actively, describe feelings.
Academic Skills: Understanding an animal and imagining its characteristics.
Teacher: Reproduce one story for each pair.

A TRADITIONAL STORY FROM THE NOOTKA

Native Americans have many traditional stories, like the *Three Bears* or *Anasi Spider*. Many of these stories of magic tell how things came to be. Raven's Beak believes that the black raven was once a white bird. After reading and discussing the story, choose a favorite animal. Talk about what the animal is like today. Make up a story about how the animal once was and why it changed into its familiar form.

THE RAVEN AND THE GREAT CHIEF

Long ago Raven was a pure white bird. He was very smart and could change himself into anything he liked. A great chief lived nearby. He kept the sun in a magic box so no one else could enjoy it or feel its warmth. Raven had a plan to trick the magician and get the sun.

The chief's daughter went to the same stream to drink every day. One day Raven changed himself into a hemlock needle and swam into the girl's cup. But the daughter was smart. She was afraid the hemlock needle might be Raven. She did not drink the water. Then Raven changed himself into a tiny grain of sand. The girl drank the water and Raven right down.

Within the daughter's body Raven changed himself into a baby boy. When he was born, the girl and her father had no idea that the baby was really Raven. He would cry and cry all the time. He was unhappy with every toy they brought him until the grandfather showed him the magic box. The chief opened it and gave the sun to Raven. Raven finally had the sun! His trick had worked!

Raven quickly changed himself back into a white bird and flew out the smoke hole of the chief's house with the sun. The smoke was sooty and colored Raven's feathers black. That is why all ravens are black today.

The great chief was very angry and used his powers to fly after Raven to get the sun back. The sun was very heavy to carry, so Raven broke off pieces of it and threw them into the sky where they became stars. Still the magician chased him. Raven broke off a bigger piece of the sun and threw it into the sky to be the moon. Finally, Raven became too tired to fly with the heavy sun. He threw it into the sky, where it has been ever since.

Social Skills: Elaborate, speak clearly, integrate a number of ideas.
Academic Skills: Verbalize and repeat a family history of a Native American tribe.
Teacher: Give each group a *Story Starter Strip.* Each develops tribal lore based on a history they agree upon or actual history of a tribe they are studying. After verbally agreeing on a story, pick one student to be the official storyteller. He or she will practice with the group until ready to tell it to others in a sharing circle.

TRIBAL LORE

Use the strips to help create your special tribal stories. Choose a group Storyteller to tell that story in Sharing Circle. Wear any of the costumes or ornaments you've designed.

Story Starter Strips:

1. **What is the name of your tribe or clan and what does it mean?**
2. **Where does your clan or tribe live and how did your come to live there?**
3. **What is your name, what does it mean, and who else is in your family?**
4. **What are the clothes you're wearing? Is there anything special about them?** **Why are they decorated in that way? Did you make them?**
5. **How did you come to be the chief or storyteller of your tribe?** **Who was the chief or storyteller before you? How did you learn the stories?**
6. **What makes your tribe or clan the bravest, best, or strongest?** **Tell a story about an exciting adventure your tribe faced.**
7. **What things does your tribe laugh at? Tell a funny story from your tribe.**
8. **What makes your tribe sad or angry? Tell a sad story about your tribe.**

Extending Activity: MORE TRIBAL LORE
Groups use other *Story Starter Strips* to continue to build unique tribal histories. Storytellers can visit other groups to tell their lore. Gather together weekly in a Sharing Circle. **Note:** Developing these stories will help groups complete the pictographs later in the book.

Social Skills: Vocalize, summarize, paraphrase.
Academic Skills: See, define, and remember words with Native American roots.
Teacher: Reproduce one *Make-a-Quiz* page for each group. Each group completes the quiz then trades papers with another group for a match-up quiz. They'll be surprised at how other children defined the words, and it's a second review for them!

NATIVE AMERICAN WORDS MAKE-A-QUIZ

All the words listed below come from tribal languages. In group discuss what each word in the list below means. Then each person takes a turn writing a definition or drawing a picture of the words next to the same number on the right. When definitions are complete, remove the scrambled numbers beside the definitions with white tape or correction fluid. Trade your quiz with another group and complete their quiz. How did the other group's definitions compare with yours?

1. **raccoon**   4.

2. **skunk**   8.

3. **moose**   6.

4. **pecan**   1.

5. **moccasin**   7.

6. **tipi**   2.

7. **toboggan**   3.

8. **totem**   5.

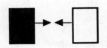

Social Skills: paraphrase, eye contact, jog memory.
Academic Skills: Learn and practice Native American picture symbols and signs.
Teacher: Reproduce one set of *Sign/Picture Co-op Cards* for each pair or group. Give the pairs time to learn and practice the symbols. Use with the *Buffalo Skin Pictographs* on page 85, and *Native American Sign Language Practice Strips* on page 84.

NATIVE AMERICAN SIGNS AND PICTURES

Practice making the hand signs and drawing the pictures for the words on the cards. You'll use them with other activities.

Sign/Picture Co-op Cards

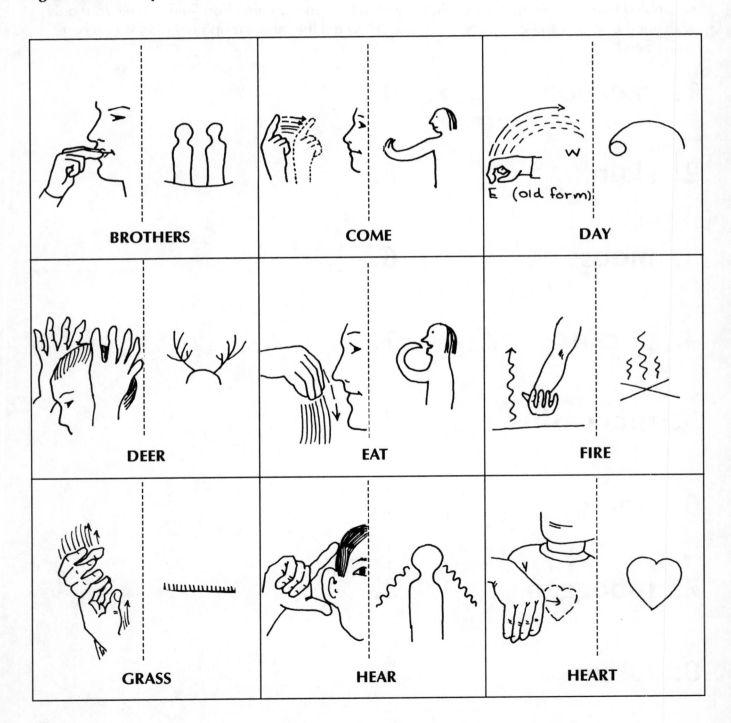

HUNGRY	**LIGHTNING**	**MANY (HEAP)**
MOON	**MOUNTAIN**	**PEACE**
RAIN	**SEE**	**SNAKE**
SUN	**TALK**	**TREE**

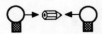

Social Skills: Participate, summarize, work toward a goal.
Academic Skills: Learn about making a written language by creating picture symbols for common words.
Teacher: Give each pair or group a different section of the *Make-a-Sign and Picture Cards* to complete. Assemble your classroom symbols to use on other pictograph assignments by making a NATIVE AMERICAN PICTURE DICTIONARY or enlarge the cards and hang them in the classroom for reference.

NATIVE AMERICAN SIGNS

Make your own co-op cards for more hand signs and pictures. Talk about how to show each word with a simple picture. Decide on a hand sign for each word. Draw how the sign is done. Draw a picture for each word. Use your cards and the others on the *Buffalo Skin Pictographs* and *Native American Sign Language Strips.*

Make-a-Sign and Picture Cards

GIRL	GO	NIGHT
BEAR	SLEEP	HAPPY
CORN	DANCE	WALK

More Make-a-Sign and Picture Cards

Complete these cards to use with the *Buffalo Skin Pictographs* on page 85 and *Native American Sign Language Strips* on page 84.

SING	BUFFALO	THIRSTY
SNOW	HORSE	TIPI
UNDERSTAND	QUESTION	HUNT

Extending Activity: NAME YOUR PARTNER

Teacher: Have partners give each other appropriate Indian names and practice signing and writing them. Some common boys' names would be Walking Bear, Running Deer, Two Moons. Girls' names might be Sun Girl (Woman), Rain in Her Hair, Peaceful Heart.

Social Skills: Vocalize, paraphrase, jog memory.
Academic Skills: Learn how to use Native American sign language.
Teacher: This activity gets children used to the way Native Americans do sign language and build picture stories. Reproduce one sheet for each pair.

NATIVE AMERICAN SIGN LANGUAGE

Cut these strips in half and practice reading and signing them with a partner. Use the co-op cards to help you with the signs.

1. Look, it is snowing!	LOOK SNOW.
2. I eat with my father.	WITH MY FATHER, I EAT.
3. I am hunting bear.	I HUNT BEAR.
4. Children love to sing and dance.	LITTLE GIRL HAPPY SING DANCE.
5. We have lived here ten years.	TEN SNOW ME-ALL SIT TIPI HERE.
6. Do you like to walk in the woods?	QUESTION YOU HAPPY GO FOREST?
7. Do you see the starving buffalo?	QUESTION YOU SEE HUNGRY BUFFALO?
8. Did you catch a deer in the forest?	QUESTION YOU HUNT DEER FOREST?
9. Do you like to eat corn?	QUESTION YOU HAPPY EAT CORN?
10. Will the bear dance bring rain?	QUESTION BEAR DANCE RAIN COME?

Social Skills: Work toward a goal, paraphrase, integrate ideas.
Academic Skills: Recognize steps toward a written language. Work out a story in pictures and symbols.
Teacher: Groups create a picture story. Reproduce one *Buffalo Skin Pattern* for each group. Use the *Co-op cards* and *Classroom Picture Dictionaries* you've made for reference in making the stories.

BUFFALO SKIN PICTOGRAPHS

Pictographs are the word pictures on the co-op cards. Write a Native American pictograph story on this skin. Decide on a story together and then take turns drawing the symbols. Begin in the center and draw your pictures in a circle to the left.

Buffalo Skin Pattern

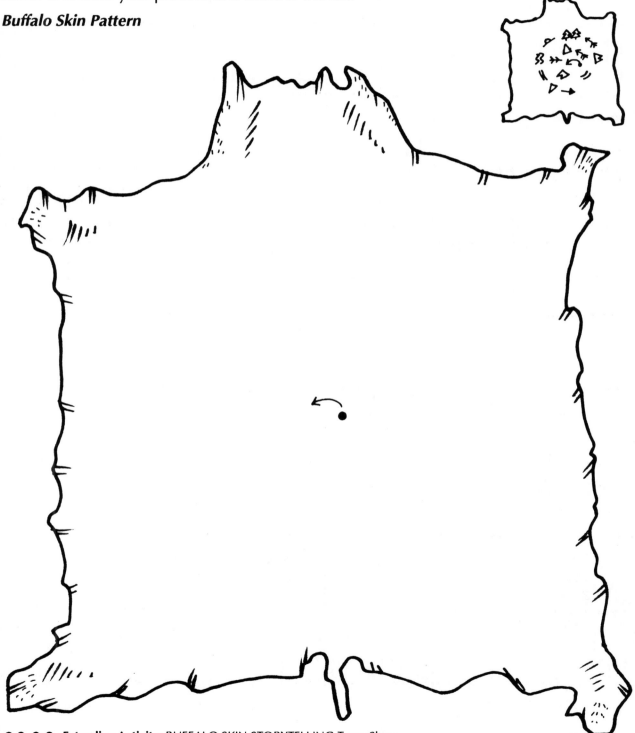

Extending Activity: BUFFALO SKIN STORYTELLING Team Share
Have your group learn the sign language for your story and practice telling it aloud with the movements, then with signs alone.

 **Social Skills:** Time limit, summarize, extend another's answers.
Academic Skills: Use a grid to create beading patterns that can convey wampum messages.
Teacher: Reproduce one *Wampum Grid* for each pair. They will each practice some designs on scrap paper, then combine their ideas for a final message.

GRAPH PAPER WAMPUM BELTS

Work out your designs in purple crayon on scrap paper. Then combine your ideas to make a special message on this wampum belt. Use some of the symbol ideas below.

Wampum Grid

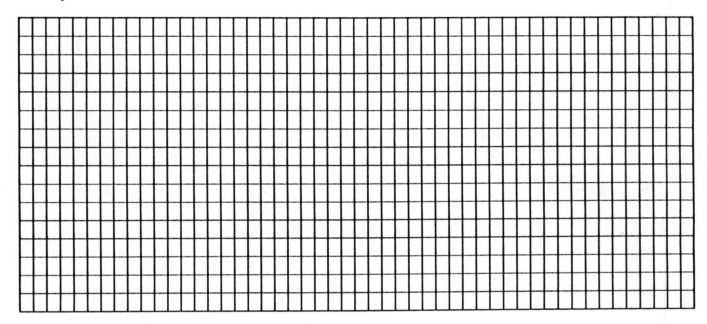

Wampum Grid Ideas

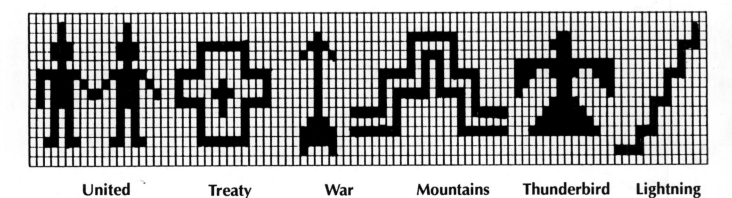

| United | Treaty | War | Mountains | Thunderbird | Lightning |

 Extending Activity: WAMPUM LIBRARIANS Interview
Have one class member (or group) learn the significance of all the wampum belts. Put them in a "library." Other classmates can ask about them and sign them out to copy and read.

Social Skills: Elaborate, speak clearly, integrate a number of ideas.
Academic Skills: Recognize the order and significance of totem symbols.
Teacher: Reproduce a number of each of the *Totem Design Patterns*. Members choose what they need for their group. Encourage groups to add other details or make more symbols to complete their pole.

BUILD-A-TOTEM

Totem Assembly:

- •. Use a paper towel roll core as a base.
- • Color and cut out your totem design. Cut the slits carefully.
- • Slide the symbols onto your pole in the order your group agrees upon.
- • Use the finished totem to tell your clan history.

Totem Design Patterns

BEAR

Cut and open slit.
Slide onto roll, bottom part behind.

KILLER WHALE

Cut and open slit.
Slide onto roll, bottom part behind.

RAVEN

Cut and open slit.
Slide onto roll, bottom part behind.

FAMILY

Cut and open slit.
Slide onto roll, bottom part behind.

 Extending Activity: TOTEM Tell-All
Be ready to show and tell about your group's totem figures and tribal symbols.

CHAPTER 5:
NATIVE AMERICAN FESTIVALS AND GAMES

To the Teacher: Every tribe of Native Americans has its own series of festivals and ceremonies throughout the year. Priests, chiefs, warriors, and storytellers guide the people through sacred ceremonies that tell of the relationships between the earth and the people. They believe the earth, air, water, and sky belong to everyone and should be saved for everyone to enjoy. You may want to read stories or listen to tapes about tribal ceremonies to learn more about how they are performed and what they mean to Native Americans. Only Native Americans should participate in these sacred rituals for their tribes.

Most festivals and ceremonies include feasting and games for fun and sport. Lacrosse is a Native American game. Children play games for fun and to practice hunting skills. This chapter has instructions for making and playing Native American games in small and large groups. As a culminating activity for your study of Native Americans you may want to have a small classroom feast using some of the recipes in chapter 3. After the feast, groups can share the games they have made to celebrate all they have learned about Native Americans.

 **Social Skills:** Work quietly, integrate ideas into one, ask for help when needed.
Academic Skill: Plan and make a Native American game.
Teacher: Reproduce one game direction sheet for each team.

PUGASAING
stick dice game

Stick dice are two-sided pieces of wood, bone, or horn. There are many different styles and designs for them. Make the stick dice and play the game with another team.

Stick Dice
Materials:
3 wooden tongue depressors
nontoxic red and black paints
paintbrush

Preparing to Play:
Partner 1: Paint designs on one side of each stick with red paint. Allow to dry.
Partner 2: Using black paint, paint designs on the other side of each stick. Allow to dry.

To Play:
Two teams of two players each take turns throwing the dice. The first player tosses the dice on the floor. The score depends on how the dice fall. See the chart to count score. Teams and players continue taking turns throwing the dice until one team gets twenty points.

sample designs for stick dice

SCORING PUGASAING
Three black sides up = 3 points
Three red sides up = 2 points
Two black and one red = 1 point
Two red and one black = 0 points

 # MOCCASIN GUESSING GAME
for two teams of two players each

Materials: 4 mini moccasins from page 31, four smooth stones, paint or marker
Preparing to Play: Mark one of the stones with paint or marker to make it different from the others. Put the moccasins in the center of a table with players sitting around it.
Play: One player takes the four stones, shakes them in his hands, and puts one stone in each moccasin. While putting in the stones, the player and his teammate try to distract the other team from seeing in which moccasin the different stone is placed. They do this by making funny faces, singing a song, or telling a joke. A person on the opposing team guesses which moccasin has the different stone. If correct, the other team tries to fool the team again. If wrong, the opposing team drops the stones in the moccasins in the same manner. The first team to guess correctly four times wins the game.

Social Skills: Work quietly, jog memory, vocalize.
Academic Skills: To learn to recognize and form star groups.
Teacher: Reproduce the game directions and *Star Groups* for each group. Provide the dried beans and peas. For extended play of the game children may want to research other star groups.

STAR GROUPS GAME

Many Native Americans can look at the sky and recognize the positions of the planets, stars, and constellations. Chiefs teach children what they know about the star groups with this game.

Star Groups

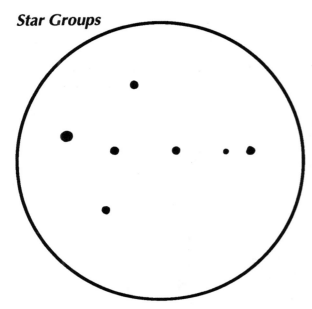

Star Group 1: Cygnus (Flying Swan)

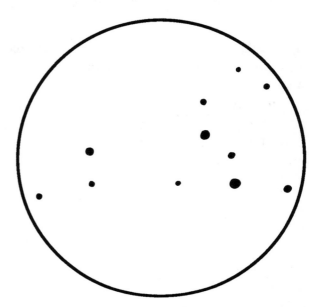

Star Group 2: Leo (Resting Lion)

Materials:
Star Groups
Dried lima beans
Dried split peas
Dried navy beans
3 sheets of dark blue paper

Preparing to Play: Cut out the Star Groups. Everyone in the group looks at and discusses each Star Group. Look at how they are positioned. Some stars are larger than others. Learn to name each group by how it looks and the sizes of the stars in it.

Play: One player is the chief and holds the Star Group cards. The other players each get a piece of blue paper and a number of beans in various sizes. When the chief names a star group, the players place beans on the blue paper to show how the Star Group named looks. Players lay down the beans from memory of how the Star Group looks. The first to correctly complete the Star Group becomes chief for another round. **Note:** When everyone in the group knows the Star Groups, look in astronomy books and find others to learn. Play the game again using the new Star Groups.

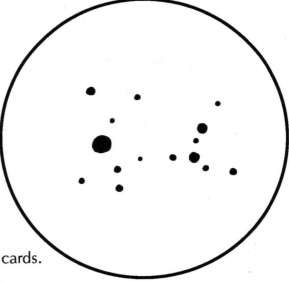

Star Group 3: Canis Major
(Big Dog)

91

Social Skills: Form groups quietly, participate, work toward a goal.
Academic Skills: To make game pieces and to learn play the Indian game Kuntassoo
Teacher: Reproduce the *Kuntassoo Game Board* on tagboard for each group. Provide the other materials.

KUNTASSOO

Sioux women develop the game and make all the game pieces. They use fruit pits for the dice. The little lines on the trail of the game board are streams that must be jumped across to go down the trail. Work together to make the game and play it.

Materials:
2 clean fruit pits (peach or prune)
4 small stones
paintbrush
nontoxic paint in four colors
1 Kuntassoo Game Board
markers or crayons

Preparing to Play:
1. Paint white dots on the fruit pits to make the dice. Paint two dots on one side of one pit and three on the other side.
2. Paint three dots on one side of the other pit and four on the other side.
3. Paint each of the stones a different color.
4. Cut out the Kuntassoo Game Board. Color it.

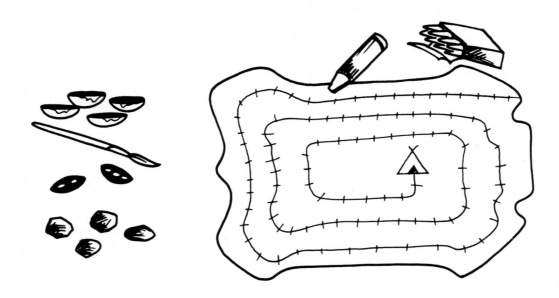

KUNTASSOO

for four players

Object of the Game: To jump streams around the trail and be the first player to reach the tipi.
Play: Each player gets a different color stone to use as a counter on the game board. The first player places his or her stone between the first two streams, shakes the dice, and tosses them on the game board. Move the stone counter around the trail the same number of spaces shown on the dice. Any time the dots add up to seven, the turn is lost and the player must return to the starting position. Players take turns tossing the dice and moving along the game board. The first to reach the tipi is the winner.

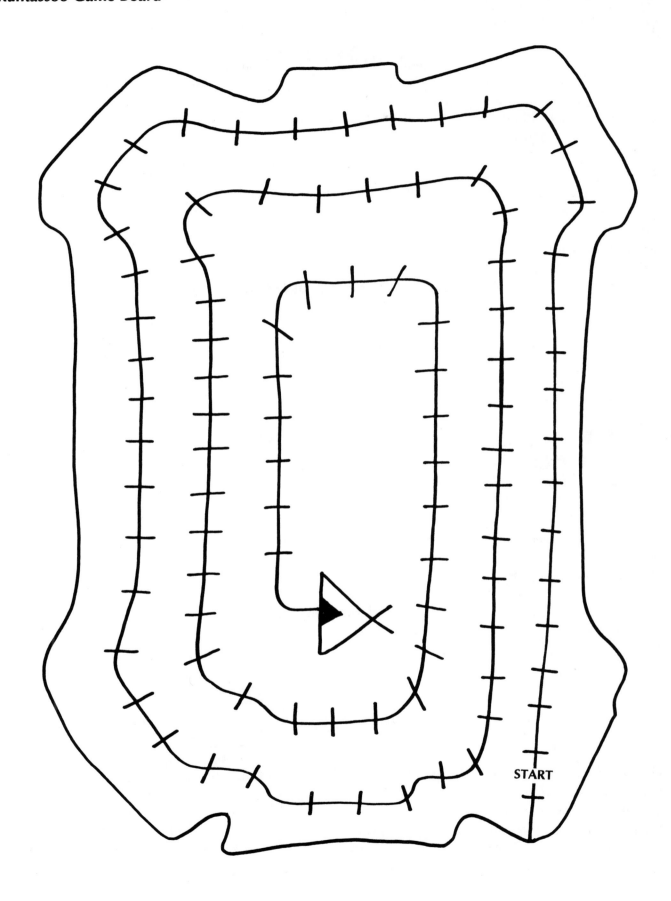

START

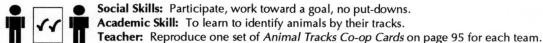

Social Skills: Participate, work toward a goal, no put-downs.
Academic Skill: To learn to identify animals by their tracks.
Teacher: Reproduce one set of *Animal Tracks Co-op Cards* on page 95 for each team.

ANIMAL TRACKS GAME

Boys learn how to hunt at an early age. Chiefs help them learn what animal they are tracking by the footprints the animals leave in the dirt or snow on the trail.

Getting Ready to Play: Cut out the Co-Op Cards. Study the cards together and learn to name the animals by their tracks. The number code below will help you.

To Play: (for two players) One player mixes up the cards and lays them face down in a pile. The first player picks up one card, looks at the tracks, and names the animal. If correct, the player keeps the card. If incorrect, the card is placed on the bottom of the pile. Taking turns, each player picks one card and tries to name the animal it represents. The game is over when all the cards have been named. The player with the most cards begins the next game.

Happy tracking!

ANIMAL TRACKS NUMBER CODE

1. deer	5. bobcat	9. otter
2. beaver	6. black bear	10. skunk
3. rabbit	7. raccoon	11. opossum
4. coyote	8. porcupine	12. fox

WOODPECKER

Preparing to Play: Indians in the Northeast play this game by throwing pinecones in a hole in a tree trunk. They say that a woodpecker has returned to its nest every time a pinecone goes into the hole. If you do not have pinecones, make some by wadding up pieces of brown grocery bags. Make the tree trunk from a large cardboard box. Cut a 4" square hole in the lid of the box and tape the lid down securely. Stand the box on its side on a table so that the hole is facing outward.

Play: (for two or more players) Players stand about 4' away from the tree trunk. The first player tries to toss a pinecone into the hole in the tree trunk. If he or she misses the next person takes a turn. When a pinecone hits the target and goes into the box, that player continues to throw until he or she misses. When the target becomes easy to hit, put the box on a higher shelf and move back a step or two.

Animal Tracks Co-op Cards

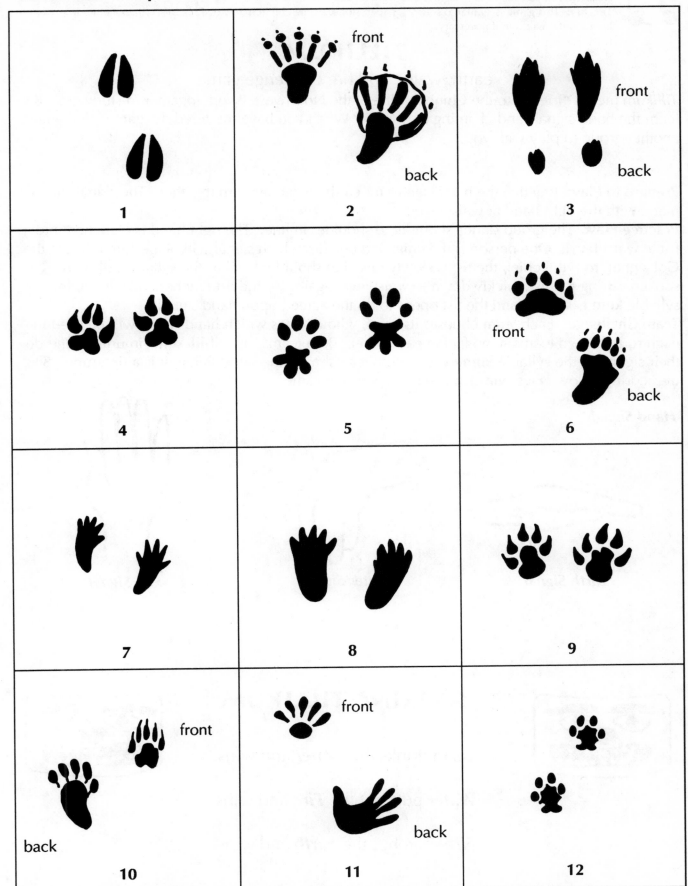

Social Skills: Quiet voices, no put-downs.
Academic Skills: Learn hand signals and work together in rhythm.
Teacher: This game is similar to scissors, paper, stone. Some children may need help staying together in rhythm. Beat it out on a drum if necessary.

TILLIKUM

earth, water, and fire challenge game

Tillikum means "friend" to the Chinook tribe of the Northwest. Work together in study groups to learn the hand signals and chanting in rhythm. When you have mastered the game, challenge another group to play with you.

Prepare to Play: Practice the hand signals for earth, water, and fire together. The signals are made with the right hand at waist level.

Practice Play: The group stands shoulder to shoulder in line. The right hand is clenched into a fist at waist level. One person is the chief and decides which signal will be performed. On the Go! signal from the chief, the fist is slowly raised to shoulder level as the syllables **til-li** are spoken. Bring the fist quickly down to waist level again. As the fist reaches waist level, the syllable **kum** is spoken and the fist opens to do the agreed-upon hand signal.

Team Challenge: Each team chooses its chief, who decides which hand signal will be used in each round. Two teams stand facing each other. Both teams say "**til-lil-kum**" in unison and do their signal on the syllable **kum**. When both teams make the same signal, it is a tie round. See the scoring below. Five wins for one team wins the game.

Hand Signals

Earth Signal

Water Signal

Fire Signal

SCORING TILLIKUM

Earth drinks the **Water** and wins.

Water puts out the **Fire** and wins.

Fire scorches the **Earth** and wins.

OUTDOOR GAMES

BUFFALO SKIN

Preparing to Play: Cut out the buffalo skin.

Play: (for eight to twenty players) This game is much like a huge Tug of War game. One player is named chief. Players join hands in a big circle with the buffalo skin in the center. When the chief shouts "Pull," all players pull and tug trying to get their opponents to touch the buffalo skin with a foot or any other part of the body. When a player touches the skin, he is out of the game until the next round.

BEAR RACE

Preparing to Play: Practice walking like a bear. With hands on the ground move the left hand and the right foot forward at the same time. Then the right hand and left foot are moved forward together. When bear-walking is mastered, the game is ready for play. Mark a starting line on the ground. Mark a finish line on the ground about 20' away.

Play: (for teams of four) Teams line up behind the starting line. At a signal the first player on each team bear-walks to the finish line. The next player follows until all team members have crossed the finish line.

RATTLESNAKE STALKER

Materials: 2 blindfolds, small cardboard box, dried peas or pebbles, masking tape

Preparing to Play: Put a few dried peas or pebbles in the box and tape it securely to seal.

Play: (for teams of two each) One team stands 6' apart within a circle of the other teams waiting for their turn to play. Both team members in the circle are blindfolded, with the ears left uncovered. One is the stalker and one is the rattler. The rattler is given the box. At a signal, the rattler shakes the box three times, about ten seconds apart as he moves around within the circle. The stalker tries to find the rattler by listening carefully for the rattles. The rattler tries to evade the stalker by listening for his footsteps. Neither may move out of the circle of other players. If they do, the game is stopped and begins again at the starting position. If the stalker is moving away from the rattler, players in the circle shout "Rattle" and the rattler must shake his rattle again. The stalker is given three minutes to try to touch the rattler. Then another pair in the circle gets to try their listening and stalking skills.

AN OVERVIEW OF COOPERATIVE LEARNING

What makes cooperative learning unique?
In a cooperative classroom, group activities are more than just children working together. Learning structures (called recipes here) guide children to respond to and interact with each other in specific ways. Every task has both an academic and social goal, which are evaluated at the end of the activity with self-monitoring as well as teacher observation.

Instead of competition, students working together learn positive interdependence, that they sink or swim together. Each student contributes their part to each activity or assignment. Each team gets a single grade based on all the members doing their part. Instead of a few top students being the stars, all members must learn and use the information for the group to be successful. Students even take on the role of instructor, presenting new material or helping teammates practice skills.

The benefits of cooperative learning:
In a cooperative classroom, you become a facilitator to learning, not the prime source of instruction. Students begin to see their classmates as important and valuable sources of knowledge. Essential interpersonal social skills learned step by step and reinforced in every lesson make the classroom climate more positive, more nurturing as students learn to give each other encouragement and praise.

Students even benefit academically, because in a cooperative atmosphere they have more chances to understand the material through oral rehearsal, thinking out loud, and discussing their views with others in the class. Contact with others' views and ideas increases their tolerance of various learning styles and personal views. Children learn that their differences make for a stronger team.

CLASSROOM GUIDELINES
GROUPING AND SOCIAL SKILLS

Planning for grouping and social skills:
Lessons have been planned for you so that the academic and social skills are built into the activity. This way, even if you have not worked with cooperative learning before, you can organize your groups quickly, spending your time monitoring and evaluating social progress.

Team groupings will be suggested for the activities. Primary classrooms work best in pairs because it is easier for children to decide or agree with one other person. Once they are working well in pairs, advance to threes and then two sets of pairs to make four. Unless your project demands it (such as a culminating activity having five or six distinct parts), four is the suggested upper limit for groups.

When choosing pairs, you may want to choose randomly or assign pairs to mix abilities and temperaments. Occasionally, you will find an oil-and-water pair, or a child who has trouble working with any partner and needs to be changed frequently. Once you have groups of four, make sure they are heterogeneous and have ample opportunity to "gel" as a group and learn to work together. Resist the temptation to break up groups who are having problems. Emphasize the social skills they need to learn and practice to get them all working together.

Defining and developing social skills:

Many teachers shy away from a group approach because they think of all the problems associated with groups of children working together: confusion, noise, personality conflicts, differences of opinion, etc. Cooperative teaching does not assume children have the social skills needed to work together successfully. The behaviors that enhance group progress are introduced, explained, modeled, practiced, and evaluated like any other skill.

To use cooperative learning successfully, it is important for you to be aware of the social skills appropriate for each activity. Introduce them at the beginning of each lesson, define, reinforce, and evaluate them at the completion of the assignment. As your groups develop, you may want to emphasize and build on other social skills of your choice. With older groups (grades 4–5), co-op activities are the ideal vehicle to experiment with learning and problem-solving skills. You can introduce these along with the simpler social skills.

These are the Interpersonal Group skills necessary in grades 1–5:

COMING TOGETHER (grades 1–5)
- form groups quietly
- stay in the group
- use quiet voices
- participate
- use names, make eye contact
- speak clearly
- listen actively
- allow no put-downs

WORKING TOGETHER (grades 1–5)
- work toward goal, purpose, time limit
- praise others, seek others' ideas
- ask for help when needed
- paraphrase other members' contributions
- energize group
- describe one's feelings when appropriate

LEARNING TOGETHER (grades 3–5)
- summarize material
- seek accuracy by correcting, giving information
- elaborate
- jog memory of teammates
- explain reasons for answers/beliefs
- plan aloud to teach concepts, agree on approaches

PROBLEM-SOLVING SKILLS (grades 4–5)
- criticize ideas, not people
- differentiate where there is disagreement
- integrate a number of ideas into a single conclusion
- ask for justification
- extend another's answer by adding to it
- probe by asking questions
- generate further answers
- check answers/conclusions with original instruction

Teaching social skills:

- Work on one social skill at a time. Add others slowly as groups are ready.
- Introduce the skill and discuss why it is important.
- Define in words and actions what children will see and hear as they are using that skill in their groups. Look through the materials in the classroom management sections to find charts, handouts, and other materials to help to do this.
- Give a demonstration for the children to follow (modeling).
- Set up practice situations and refer to the charts, etc., as children practice the skill.
- Praise lavishly attempts to use a skill, repeat words/deeds done showing it.
- At the end of the session, give children time to think whether they used the skill in the session or not. Evaluate them by the use of the teacher charts provided or have them vote as a group as to whether they think they succeeded and why.
- Be patient with yourself and the students. Social skills need to be practiced often to become natural.

COOPERATIVE GUIDELINES: PREPARING LESSONS

Along with the team grouping suggestions, cooperative recipes for learning (sometimes called practice structures) are used with the activities in this book. The symbol for the recipe is clearly shown on each lesson. The academic and social skills to be emphasized are beside each symbol. This will help you to organize the class and choose the lessons you wish to use.

The recipes provided each reinforce a number of social skills and guide children to process information in their groups in a variety of ways. For the first time through the materials, we suggest you use the recipe with one or two of the social skills listed near the symbol for each activity. However, when you are familiar with the projects, you can emphasize other skills. It is our hope that you will make the lessons your own, adapting them to your particular classroom. As you work through each, they will become natural to you and your students. They will make a positive impact on your classroom atmosphere and student performance. The key is to be patient and give children time to learn and practice each recipe.

COOPERATIVE CLASSROOM RECIPES

Sharing Circle

Social skills: Listen actively, participate, clear speech

Group size: Whole class

Directions: Children sit in a large circle, so each student can see the rest. The leader (teacher or student) starts an open-ended statement or sentence, and each student in turn ends it with their own statement. If they can't think of an answer at that time, they can pass, but are expected to have their answer ready by the time the circle is completed.

Study Group

Social skills: paraphrasing, positive support, time limit, group purpose

Group size: 2–4

Directions: Present information in a traditional way. Children get into their small groups to complete a cooperative assignment that reinforces, expands on, or tests their knowledge. Groups can brainstorm, fill out a K W L chart within their groups to set goals for further study or complete various activities like word webbing.
Note: Use the role cards and discussion strips to help keep social skills moving while in groups. Another quick associations recipe is **Numbered Heads Together.**

Numbered Heads Together

Social skills: Use quiet voices, participate, time limit, quick associations, elaborate, integration, team energizing, and praise

Group Size: 2–4

Note: For this activity, you will need a code or signal to get all the groups attention: lights on/off, a bell, or hand signal. Use it with other recipes as needed.

Directions: Students are in groups, listening to instruction by teacher. When a question is posed, the teacher tells the groups to put their heads together and discuss it. This gives students a chance to immediately discuss the information and figure out the right response together. After a time is given for discussion, the teacher signals for attention. At this time, students number off within each group. The teacher calls one number, and a representative from each group gives the team's answer. Team points are given for correct responses.

Note: If you want simultaneous responses, have team members write their response on a card and hold it up, or write their solution on the blackboard.

Turn to Your Partner

Social skills: Using names, eye contact, listen actively, quiet voices, paraphrasing

Group size: 2

Directions: As you present material, have students pair up to share ideas, information, or opinions. This works best when you use established partners who sit near each other already, in order to minimize the amount of class time spent on moving toward partners. It is a good way to quickly reinforce active listening and early social skills.

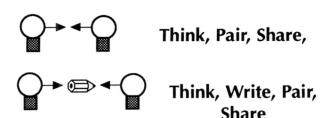

Think, Pair, Share,

Think, Write, Pair, Share

Social skills: Paraphrasing, memory of content, vocalization

Group size: 2

Directions: Similar to Turn to Your Partner, but when more time is wanted on task. Present material, have students pair up to think about the content just presented, share ideas, information or opinions. This works well when you use established partners, but can also be used to exchange pairs to get different opinions. If you have children write down their idea (and it is a good idea, so they won't be swayed or lose direction), you can pair them up with others who think the same thing or have different opinions.

Note: For another way to group by opinion or interest, see Pick Your Spot.

Pick Your Spot (Corners)

Social skills: Vocalization, groups by interest or opinion

Group size: 4–6
Note: By having children write down responses ahead of time, they will stay on task better and get to their places quicker. You can see where they're headed and direct them to the right corner.
Directions: Pose a question or topic with four answers or subtopics and have each child select which of the four would be their choice. Have them write it down and go to the corner of the room where that topic or answer is displayed. This is a quick way to get children with similar interests together to do further study, share opinions, or become roving reporters to teach the rest of the class.

Note: For another way to group children by interest or opinion see Line-Ups.

Line-Ups

Social skills: Vocalization, probing for information, sharing reasons for answer

Group size: Whole class or split in half for two lines
Note: This works best in probing an answer or problem with a range of opinions.

Directions: Create a masking tape line on your classroom floor divided into three categories; yes/maybe/no, always/sometimes/never, etc. Pose a question or situation. Have the children write down their answer on small slips of paper. Then have them line up on the line that nearest matches their opinion. Once they're on the line, you can use the information by having them discuss with their immediate group their reasons for choosing that answer or leave their paper markers in place and go back to their desks to look and compare how many are in each section and make a class opinion graph. Some classroom teachers have developed lively discussions by having the children pair with members from other sections to discuss why they thought differently. The line can remain in place to be used later.

Stand and Share

Social skills: Speak clearly, listen actively, participate, time limit

Group size: 2–4

Directions: As in Study Group, teams ready themselves on a specific topic. Teams or members within each team number off. When the teacher calls a number, all the team members must stand and be ready to answer the question. As you call the numbers, that team or member answers the questions and sits down. This is good for an oral quiz or checking problems where all members need to know the information.

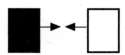

Co-op Cards

Social skills: Using names, eye contact, positive statements, jog memory

Group size: Do first with partners, then in groups of 4.

Note: This format is an invaluable method for memory work and drill; children learn while praising each other and supporting each other's efforts.

Directions: Give each pair or study group a set of the Co-op Cards you want them to learn. Have them learn to play these games:

Game 1: Maximum Help
Partner 1 hands his card to partner 2. Partner 2, the teacher, shows the cards and the answers one by one, to Partner 1, the student, who repeats the words or answers. Cards done correctly are won back with lots of praise from the teacher. Cards done incorrectly are repeated and explained thoroughly by the tutor and asked again. When all cards are won back, they switch roles.

Game 2: Minimum Help
Partner 1 hands his card to partner 2. Partner 2, the teacher, shows the cards one by one to partner 1, the student, who answers. Cards done correctly are won back with lots of praise from the teacher. Cards done incorrectly are repeated with some hints. When all cards are won back, they switch roles.

Game 3: No Help
Partner 1 hands his card to partner 2. Partner 2, the teacher, shows the cards one by one to partner 1, the student, who answers. Cards done correctly are won back with lots of praise from the teacher. Cards done incorrectly are put back into the teacher's stack to be repeated with no hints. When all cards are won back, they switch roles.

Evaluation: Groups can keep a chart showing all words learned, with an envelope for those words that still need to be practiced and won.

Note: To keep the game fresh, the teacher should continually think of new and grander praises.

Pairs Check or Partners

Social skills: Accuracy, energizing, positive support, ways to jog memory

Group size: 2

Directions: Teams work in pairs. In each pair, one player does a problem. The other is the coach in every sense of the word, giving help, praise, and encouragement! Switch roles after every problem. When two problems are completed, pairs must check with each other and agree on the answers. This is a good time to have a team handshake. Then proceed to the next two problems in the same way. Remember to keep your pairs heterogeneous for activities like this, so there is a range of abilities to keep things moving.

Interview

Social skills: Using names, eye contact, paraphrasing, summarizing, describing feelings, probing for answers, vocalization

Group size: 3–4

Note: This format is good to prepare for a unit or to close a unit.

Directions: Members take turns interviewing each other. After they have all had a chance to share, have the group round-robin (described at right) what they learned from the interviews. For example, each child could take on one of the characters from an event or story and give his or her perspective. Use of role cards or discussion strips, so each asks a pertinent question, will help it go more smoothly.

Roundtable

Social skills: Time limit, quick associations, participate, extend another's answers

Group size: 3–4

Directions: All team members contribute ideas to one sheet of paper. Make sure the team members know the directions the paper should be passed. When the signal is given, members write or draw the answer and pass it on.

Simultaneous Roundtable

Social skills: time limit, waiting politely, quiet voices, participate

Directions: More than one sheet is passed within the group. Members start with one sheet each and pass it on.

Round Robin

Social skills: Vocalization, time limit, quick associations, participate, extend another's answers, building team spirit

Group size: 3–4

Directions: This is an oral counterpart to Roundtable. **Note:** This is an excellent method for brainstorming vocabulary, problem solving, or creating an oral story together. It is also excellent for younger students with limited writing skills.

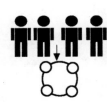

Team Share

Social skills: Planning to teach, elaborate, vocalization, ways to jog memory, extend another's answers, integrate a number of ideas

Group size: 3–4

Note: This is an ideal way to have teams share products or projects with each other. Be sure to give teams time to plan how they will present themselves.

Directions: When teams have completed various projects, have them get ready to share with other teams. Organize the class so each team is clearly marked and knows where they are to go. For instance, a blue #1 card goes to one team, a blue #2 card goes to another, and they meet at the blue station. Team #1 shares first, team #2 is the audience. Then they switch. If you have an uneven number of teams, you can pair up with one or put three groups together.

CLASSROOM MANAGEMENT CHARTS AND BUTTONS

These materials will help you define, display, and reinforce social lessons.

Standards T-Chart

To use: Enlarge and reproduce full-page or poster-size. Write the social skill to be learned in the top section as you discuss its importance. Have your classes brainstorm how it looks when children are using that skill, as well as how it sounds when it's happening. This gives the children a solid basis for modeling and monitoring their social behavior. Display it prominently and refer to it often. Laminate and save. Use the chart whenever that skill is being emphasized.

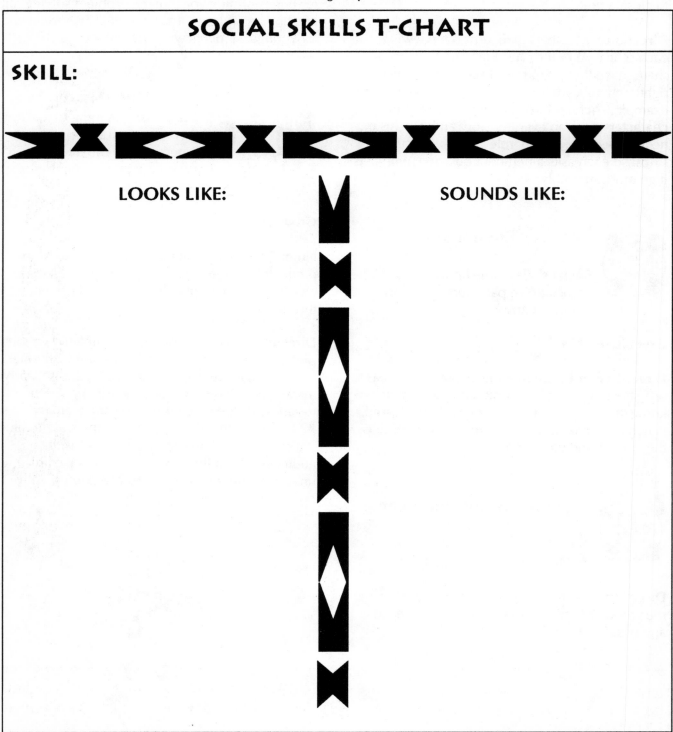

SOCIAL SKILLS T-CHART

SKILL:

LOOKS LIKE: **SOUNDS LIKE:**

PRAISE WORDS

To use: In order to increase the kind and frequency of encouraging words in the classroom, brainstorm suggestions and write them in open areas within the Native American design. Keep them on display. As you hear others, add them to the chart with plenty of praises of your own.

TALK TO OTHERS AS YOU WOULD HAVE THEM TALK TO YOU.

Note: For a class with ingrained negative habits, it may also be helpful to put up a list of TABOO or OFF-LIMITS sayings. These can be placed on another chart with a line through them or the title "Cooperative NO-NOs!"

DISCUSSION STRIPS

To use: Reproduce the strips you will use on as many different colors of paper as there are members of each team. Each student gets appropriate strips to use during group discussions. Whenever a student contributes, a strip is "spent." Discussion goes on until all have used their strips. This keeps all members contributing equally, and aware of *how* they are responding. **Note:** Younger groups may need practice in many of these modes before it comes naturally to them, so start simply. Have each child bring an envelope from home to store the strips in for later use.

ANSWER A QUESTION	**ASK A QUESTION**
CHECK FOR UNDERSTANDING	**ENCOURAGE YOUR GROUP**
GIVE A PRAISE WORD	**GIVE AN IDEA**
KEEP YOUR GROUP ON TASK	**PARAPHRASE**
RESPOND TO AN IDEA	**SUMMARIZE PROGRESS**

EVALUATION TOOLS

TEACHER OBSERVATION FORM

To use: When your groups are working, use this form as you circulate, observe, and record their progress. Be sure to write quotes and repeat them to further reinforce and model behavior during and after the activity.

TEACHER OBSERVATION CHART

SKILL: _____

GROUP	STUDENTS	COMMENTS

K-W-L CHART

To use: Have the children discuss an upcoming topic and fill in questions for the K, W, and L sections. Reproduce full-page size for use in the small groups to focus learning or poster-size as a whole-class exercise to introduce a topic.

K= What I KNOW about: _____.
W= WHAT I would like to find out: _____.
L= What I have LEARNED: _____.

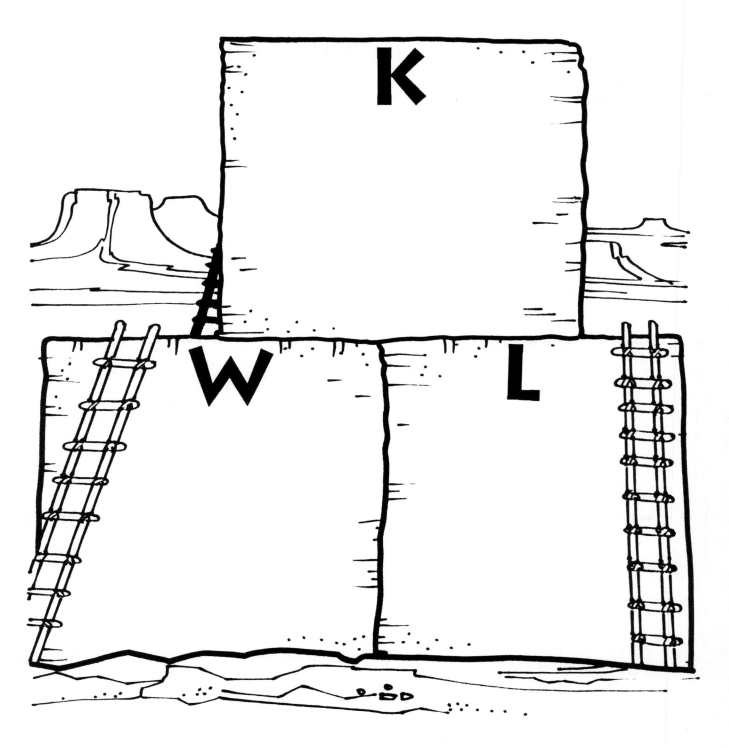

ROLE BUTTONS

To use: Reproduce on sturdy tagboard and cut out. When children are doing group work, it may help them to have a visual reminder of their group job. Use those applicable to the activity and supply them to the groups. You will also find it easier to check if students are performing as they should because you can see at a glance what each member's role is within the group.

CHEERLEADER
Energize the team with positive comments and support.

CHECKER
Make sure everyone agrees.

GATEKEEPER
Make sure all participate equally.

ENCOURAGER
Praise individual and team efforts.

RECORDER
(secretary)
Write down team answers.

TASK MASTER
Make sure team is accomplishing established goals.

QUIET CAPTAIN
Make sure team doesn't disturb others.

GROUP EVALUATION FORM

To use: Take a few minutes after an activity for teams or individuals to evaluate their progress. The group form should be agreed upon by members, filled in, and initialed by all. The individual form will be helpful when groups are having problems. They'll be able to spot areas needing improvement.

How Are We Doing?	How Am I Doing?
Group: _____ **Date:** _____	**Group:** _____ **Date:** _____
1. We each contributed ideas: often ___ sometimes ___ not very much ___	1. I contributed my ideas: often ___ sometimes ___ not very much ___
2. We listened to each other: often ___ sometimes ___ not very much ___	2. I listened to my partners: often ___ sometimes ___ not very much ___
3. We encouraged each other: often ___ sometimes ___ not very much ___	3. I encouraged my partners: often ___ sometimes ___ not very much ___
4. We built on each other's ideas: often ___ sometimes ___ not very much ___	4. I built on my partners' ideas: often ___ sometimes ___ not very much ___

AWARD CERTIFICATE

To use: When you see groups working and accomplishing goals, give them a visual reminder of their progress. Groups can earn them, barter them, display them with team pride, or use toward whole-class goals.

THANK YOU,

_____

FOR MAKING THIS CLASS
A FRIENDLY PLACE TO LEARN!

SIGNED _____

DATE _____

Selected Bibliography

Many materials were used in the preparation of this book. The following list should be used as a starting point. Your local librarian will help you find other appropriate materials.

American Indian Authors for Young Readers, A selected bibliography compiled by Mary Gloyne Byler (The Association on American Indian Affairs catalog)

American Indian Music for the Classroom by Louis W. Ballard (Canyon Records, 1973)

Before Columbus by Muriel Batherman (Houghton Mifflin, 1990)

Books Without Bias: Through Indian Eyes by Beverly Slapin and Doris Seale (Oyate, 1988)

Corn Is Maize by Aliki (HarperCollins, 1976)

Custer & Crazy Horse by Jim Razzi (Scholastic, 1989)

The Defenders by Ann McGovern (Scholastic, 1989)

Growing Up Indian by Evelyn Wolfson (Walker & Co. 1986)

If You Lived With the Sioux Indians by Ann McGovern (Scholastic, 1972)

Indian Chiefs by Russell Freeman (Holiday House, 1987)

Indian Summer by Barbara Girion (Scholastic, 1990)

Indians by Edwin Tunis (HarperCollins, 1979)

Iroquois Stories: Heroes and Heroines, Monsters and Magic by Joseph Bruchas (Crossing Press, 1985)

Keepers of the Earth, Native American Stories for Children by Michael Caduto (Fulcrum Publishers, 1988)

Mouse Couple retold by Ekkehart Malotki (Northland, AZ, 1988)

The Mud Pony retold by Caron Lee Cohen (Scholastic, 1988)

North American Indians by Marie and Douglas Gorsline (Random House, 1978)

Pocahontas and the Strangers by Clyde Robert Bulla (Scholastic, 1988)

Our Voices, Our Land by Indian Peoples of the Southwest, Edited by Stephen Trimble (Northland, AZ, 1988)

Sweetgrass by Jan Hudson (Scholastic, 1991)

Cooperative Learning References

Circles of Learning, Cooperation in the Classroom by David W. Johnson, Roger T. Johnson, Edythe Johnson Holubec, Patricia Roy (Association for Supervision and Curriculum Development, 1984)

Cooperative Learning: Getting Started by Susan Ellis and Susan Whalen (Scholastic Inc., 1990)

Cooperative Learning Lessons for Little Ones by Lorna Curan (Resources for Teachers, 1990)

INDEX